It's Another Ace Book from CGP

This book is for 12-14 year olds.

First we stick in all the really important stuff
you need to do well in the Key Stage Three Shakespeare Paper.

Then we have a really good stab at trying to make it funny —
so you'll actually use it.

Simple as that.

CGP are just the best

The central aim of Coordination Group Publications is to produce top quality books that are carefully written, immaculately presented and marvellously funny — whilst always making sure they exactly cover the National Curriculum for each subject.

And then we supply them to as many people as we possibly can, as cheaply as we possibly can.

Buy our books — they're ace

Contents

Section One — How To Do Well

Section Two — Understanding The Play

Section Three — Reading The Language

Section Four — The Main Characters

Section Five — Understanding The Story

Section Six — Writing About The Play

Section Seven — Example Tasks

Section Eight — The Key Scenes

Published by Coordination Group Publications Ltd.

Contributors:
Simon Cook BA (Hons)
Taissa Csáky BA (Hons)
Gemma Hallam BA (Hons)
Simon Little BA (Hons)
Glenn Rogers BSc (Hons)

Additional Contributors:
Angela Billington BA (Hons)
Chris Dennett BSc (Hons)
Iain Nash BSc
Laura Schibrowski BSc (Hons)
Claire Thompson BSc

ISBN 1-84146-149-0

Groovy website: www.cgpbooks.co.uk

Jolly bits of clipart from CorelDRAW

Printed by Elanders Hindson, Newcastle upon Tyne.

0201

Why People Hate Shakespeare

You've got to write about *Twelfth Night* for your SAT — whether you like it or not. It doesn't matter if you think it's naff or boring — just remember, it's not impossible.

Shakespeare is Dead Boring

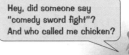

Twelfth Night isn't as boring as you might think. There's a big case of mistaken identity, some people getting their own back on a pompous pillock, everyone falling in love all over the shop, lots of singing and drunken antics, a comedy sword-fight and some cheeky cross-dressing.

Shakespeare Isn't Side-Splittingly Funny

Tak'st thou my mother-in-law. Nay, take her, I say.
Comedy
He's not as good as that Eddie Izzard.

1) A lot of Shakespeare's plays are called comedies, but people don't tend to find them that funny these days.

2) People laughed at the jokes when they were written, and some bits are still reasonably rib-tickling.

3) In your SAT, you could get asked to write about why a scene is funny. You won't get good marks if you say it's boring — you've got to answer the question.

4) You need to understand the play and say why it's supposed to be funny, whether or not you actually laugh at the jokes.

You Can't Understand What Anyone's Saying

1. The play's written in the sort of English people spoke at the time it was written. Shakespeare was a writer and poet who lived between 1564 and 1616. He wrote *Twelfth Night* around 1601. English has really changed since then.

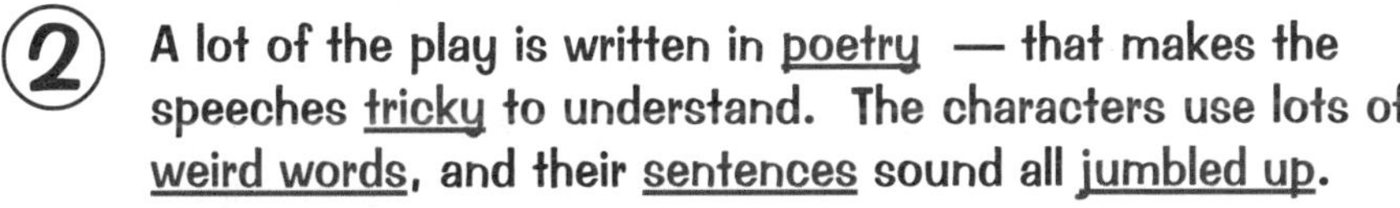

2. A lot of the play is written in poetry — that makes the speeches tricky to understand. The characters use lots of weird words, and their sentences sound all jumbled up.

"to take those things for bird-bolts that you deem cannon-bullets"

Don't give up right away — you just need to practise reading it. The more you read the play, the easier it'll get to understand.

Shakespeare's jokes — they're pretty bard...

Understanding the play — that's the hardest part. Just keep in mind that the more you read the play, the easier it'll get to understand. And that means you'll do much better in your SAT. It's up to you — stick at it and get good marks, or give up and do badly. It really is your choice.

What Happens in the Play

If you want good marks in your Paper 2, you've got to know the play well. Otherwise, it'll always be a complete mystery. If you've already read the play, use these two pages to revise.

Shipwrecks and Love Triangles — just like Titanic

You get a picture of what Orsino and Olivia are like.

1) Orsino is the Duke of Illyria. He is in love with a countess called Olivia. She isn't interested because she's still mourning the death of her brother.

2) Viola and Sebastian are twin sister and brother who look very much alike. They're shipwrecked off the coast of Illyria, and get separated. Each one thinks that the other was drowned. Viola comes ashore and disguises herself as a boy, calling herself Cesario. She gets a job as a page boy in Orsino's palace.

3) Orsino tells Viola/Cesario about his feelings for Olivia. He sends Viola/Cesario to try to persuade Olivia to change her mind. Unfortunately, Olivia falls in love with Cesario. Viola/Cesario has fallen in love with Orsino.

Blimey — things are already looking complicated.

Trapped in a cheesy love triangle!

Making a Fool of Malvolio

Er, the drinks are on me, I think.

4) Olivia's uncle, Sir Toby Belch, is a bit of a party animal who likes his drink. He's been sponging off a stupid rich knight called Sir Andrew Aguecheek. He tells Sir Andrew that Olivia might marry him. Olivia's steward, Malvolio, doesn't like Toby or Andrew, and tells them off for making too much noise one night.

5) Maria, Olivia's lady-in-waiting, hatches a plot to get revenge on Malvolio. She makes him believe Olivia is in love with him by writing a fake love letter. He believes it and goes to see Olivia dressed in silly clothes and acting outrageously. She thinks he's gone mad, and hands him over to Sir Toby, who has him locked up as a madman.

Love triangles? — I prefer octagons...

Knowing what happens in the play will help you to understand the bits you have to read. Learn these pages — well enough that you can scribble down a summary of the play from memory.

What Happens in the Play

This is where the action really gets going — make sure you learn what happens and when.

Sebastian Turns Up and It all Gets Confusing

6) In the meantime, Sebastian has been rescued by a ship's captain called Antonio. Sebastian decides to go to Orsino's court, and Antonio offers to go with him. However, Antonio has to stay in hiding because he was once involved in a war against Orsino, so Sebastian goes off on his own to explore. Antonio lends him his money.

Never fear, Antonio's here!

7) Meanwhile, Viola/Cesario keeps coming to see Olivia. Sir Andrew thinks there's something going on between Viola/Cesario and Olivia. Sir Toby forces Sir Andrew to challenge Viola/Cesario to a duel. Neither of them wants to fight, but Antonio comes along in the nick of time and rescues Viola/Cesario — he thinks she's Sebastian.

This bit is dead complicated — you need to get it clear in your head (see next page)

8) The police catch up with Antonio and arrest him. He asks Viola/Cesario for the money that he gave to Sebastian. She doesn't know what he means, but Antonio curses Sebastian — he believes that Sebastian has betrayed him. Viola/Cesario guesses that Sebastian's alive.

At the End Everyone Works Out what's Going On

9) It gets worse — Olivia meets Sebastian, and thinks he's Cesario. She tries to charm him, and he goes home with her. Next thing, they get married.

10) Orsino comes to visit Olivia. The officers bring Antonio to be judged. He claims Viola/Cesario has betrayed him, but everyone else is confused.

11) Olivia appears and says she's married to Viola/Cesario. The Duke is furious. Then Sir Toby and Sir Andrew appear and say they've been beaten up by Viola/Cesario. Finally, Sebastian arrives and everyone realises what's been going on. When the Duke finds out Viola is a woman, he realises he's in love with her and promises to marry her.

I'll get you for this!

12) Malvolio comes before the Duke. He asks Olivia why he's been treated so badly. When he shows her the letter he found, she tells him it isn't her handwriting. The trick is explained. Realising he's been made a fool of, Malvolio storms off, threatening revenge on everybody.

Shipwrecks — don't go overboard on them...

Wow, that's a lot of action... It's rather like the plot summary for some kind of weird soap opera. It's confusing at first, but stick with it. Learning these two pages really will help you.

Two Confusing Things

Here are two things that cause real confusion — get them straight in your head now.
If you don't, none of the new stuff you learn about the play will make sense.

Viola and Cesario are the Same Person

OK, it may not look difficult, but it can get really confusing with all these names floating around.

1) For most of the play, Viola is dressed up as a young boy. The only person who knows she's a woman is the captain who rescued her, and he doesn't turn up again.

2) Viola's called Cesario while she's dressed as a man. All the other characters call her Cesario when they talk about her/him. As far as they're concerned, they are talking about a man.

3) The story gets complicated when people start mistaking Viola and Sebastian for each other. It's confusing when you read the play, because the stage directions say Viola, but all the other characters call her Cesario. Best get used to it now, or it'll cause no end of trouble.

In this book, we talk about Viola/Cesario just to remind you, but if you learn this now, you won't have any problems:

Viola and Cesario are the SAME PERSON

Viola = Cesario

The Story about Malvolio is a Subplot

The main plot is everything that goes on between Viola, Olivia and Orsino, and the case of mistaken identity between Viola and Sebastian. It's the story of the play.
The plot to make a fool of Malvolio is like an extra story on the side.
It's like a soap opera — you have lots of different plots going on at the same time.

The two stories aren't totally separate, though.
The same people are involved in both stories.

Sir Toby and Sir Andrew are mostly involved in the subplot, but they get dragged into the main plot when Sir Andrew has the fight with Viola/Cesario.

Hey, are you going to stay stuck to me for, like, forever?

Having an extra story on the side isn't as much fun as it seems.

Singing in the bath — that'd be a soap opera...

This Viola/Cesario business is confusing. Just remember this — Viola and Cesario are the same person, but everyone really thinks that Viola is a bloke. The whole Malvolio trick isn't the main story.

What You've Got to Do

The whole play sounds pretty long and complicated — but don't worry about that. All you've got to do in your SAT is read one short bit from the play and do one task based on it.

You've Got to Do One Task in Your SAT

We've only got one flask,
but she's a mighty big 'un.

There'll be six tasks about Shakespeare plays in your SAT paper — you only have to do one of them. Only two tasks are about *Twelfth Night*. Ignore the rest.

The tasks are questions that ask you to write something about part of the play. You get loads of hints to help you with your answer.

Each Task has a Bit of the Play that Goes with It

1) Each task is about one particular bit of the play, and it'll tell you exactly which bit:

Act 1 Scene 1 or Act 3 Scene 5, line 37 to the end of the scene

2) As well as the question paper, you'll get a booklet with all the different bits of the plays. Find the bits from *Twelfth Night*. Don't even look at any of the other plays.

Read Both Tasks Before You Choose

There are lots of different kinds of task you could be asked to do. Don't jump in with the first one you read. Look through both of them carefully before you make your mind up.

This tells you which play the task is about...

Twelfth Night

...And this tells you which bit of the play.

Act 2 Scene 4

This sets the scene — it's here to tell you what's happening.

TASK 1

In this scene Orsino and Viola talk about love.

What do we learn about Orsino and his attitude to love?

Here's the actual task — you've got to answer this question.

Before you begin to write you should think about:

You'll also get a sentence like this, followed by some handy tips for answering the question. They're there to help you — so use them.

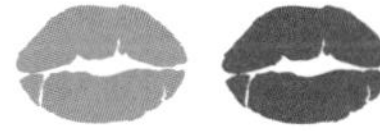

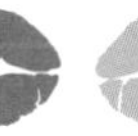
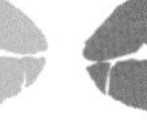

No, I said tips...

What you've got to do — An Exam, actually...

You've only got to answer one question in your Shakespeare SAT. That means it's dead important to pick the question you can do best. Read the questions carefully before you choose.

How to Get Good Marks

This is important. You've got to do all of this in your SAT. Be prepared — learn it.

You've Got to Show You Understand the Scene

This is the secret of doing well in Paper 2 — understanding the scene you're writing about. It's what you're marked on.

1 Show you Know What Happens

How does the character of Sir Andrew Aguecheek add humour to this scene?

Write about what he says, what he does, and what the other characters say about him.

Check out Section 5.

You can't write a good answer unless you know exactly what happens in the scene.

2 Show you Know What the Characters are Like

Section 4 tells you what all the characters are like.

Sir Andrew Aguecheek is foolish. In lines 46-56 he doesn't understand what Sir Toby means by "accost" and ends up looking silly. Maria thinks he is stupid: "He's a very fool and a prodigal."

You have to find bits in the scenes they give you to back up what you're saying. You need to prove you know what you're talking about.

3 Write about the Mood of the Scene

Say what it feels like to hear or read it — and how Shakespeare uses language to make you feel like that. This sounds tricky — it's really about what the scene makes you feel.

Shakespeare uses word-play to create humour in this scene. Sir Andrew doesn't realise when he's making a pun, so the audience laugh at him.

Say why you think it's funny.

A lot of things in the play seem pretty strange to us — but Section 2 has plenty of useful background bits that'll help you understand it.

A well-behaved communist — good Marx...

Understanding the scene — that's what it's all about. You have to show the examiners that you know what happens in the scene, and what the characters are like — look at Sections 4 and 5.

Writing Well & Giving Examples

Two more key things you have to do here — make sure you get them clear in your head now.

You Also Get Marked on How Well You Write

1) It's painful but true — you've got to get your spelling and punctuation perfect. They'll take marks away from you if you don't.

2) Don't forget to write in paragraphs. Every time you want to talk about a new idea, start a new paragraph.

3) Here's the tough one — try to sound interested in the play, even if you don't like it. Show the examiners that you're keen by using lots of interesting words and phrases in your answer.

Looks like you've blown it again, Tonto.

Contestants in the Appalachian Riding Tournament are marked on how well they ride, not just what they ride.

Shakespeare makes the scene comic by his brilliant use of formal language — it makes Malvolio seem very arrogant.

You've Got to Give Loads of Examples

They want you to give examples from the scene that have something to do with the task you chose. For a really good answer, you need to explain why your examples are relevant.

Don't make your examples too long. Two lines is about right.

You Can Write About Any Version of the Play You've Seen

In your answer, you can write about any version of the play you've seen. Be careful, though. You won't get extra marks just because you've seen the play. Only write about a production you've seen if it actually helps you answer the question. Don't wander off the point.

Every version has a director who decides what the costumes will look like, which actors will play the characters and how they'll say their lines.

Some directors change loads of things in the play. Any version you've seen is only one way of doing it.

No sweets between meals, kids — a sweet exterior oft hides corruption.

OK, people, we're doing it a bit differently. Viola will be played by a plate of cakes, and Rob here is playing Malvolio as a dentist.

Sometimes directors swap the first and second scenes around, so the play starts with Viola arriving on the shore of Illyria.

Sometimes they make the Malvolio story deadly serious so he really does go mad at the end.

A-version — can't say I like it much...

You're being marked on two things in your SAT — how well you read and understand the bit from the play and how well you write about it. And the secret is to give plenty of examples.

Revision Summary

Well, there it is. This first section should give you a jolly good slab of knowledge to build everything else on. It won't do you much good if you don't learn it, though. This is where these cunning Revision Summary questions come in. Do them all, don't miss any out, and keep doing them until you've got them all right. If you don't know the answers, look back through the section. Happy learning...

1) Why doesn't it matter if you don't find the play pant-wettingly funny?
2) Why isn't Olivia interested in Orsino?
3) Why do Viola and Sebastian look so similar?
4) Who does Olivia fall in love with?
5) What's Olivia's uncle called?
6) Who's his dim friend?
7) Which characters play a trick on Malvolio?
8) Does he fall for it?
9) What happens to Malvolio?
10) Who rescued Sebastian from the shipwreck?
11) Who challenges Cesario to a duel?
12) Why does Antonio ask Cesario for money?
13) Who does Olivia marry, and why?
14) When does everyone realise what's been going on?
15) What does Orsino do when he finds out that Cesario is really Viola?
16) What does Malvolio do at the end?
17) In the SAT, how many questions will there be about *Twelfth Night*?
18) How many questions do you have to answer? a) *One* b) *Two* c) *As many as you like*
19) If the task gives you four hints to "think about before you start to write," how many of the hints should you write about? a) *None of them — they're only hints* b) *One or two, just to show you care* c) *All four of them*
20) What are the three key things you need to do to get good marks?
21) Apart from understanding the scene, what else do you get marked on?
22) If you've seen a film or a stage production of *Twelfth Night*, are you allowed to write about it in the SAT?

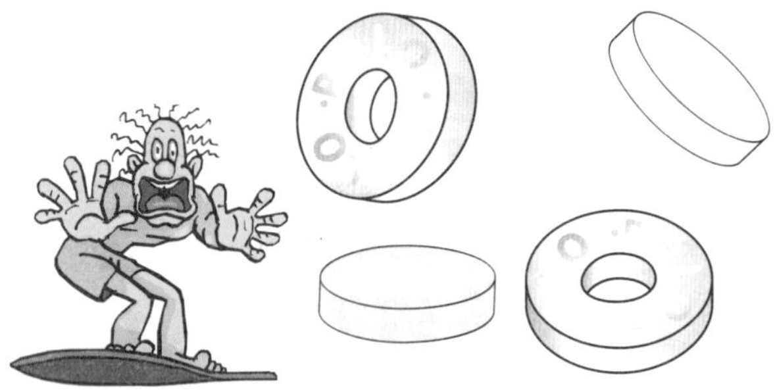

You'll get four hints.
If you get four mints, then you can start worrying.

Why the Play Seems Weird

Lots of the things that seem weird in *Twelfth Night* weren't weird when it was written. You've got to know what they are — it's the only way to answer the SAT questions properly.

Don't Forget the Play is Around 400 Years Old

Phew — that's pretty old for anything, especially a play. It's like an episode of Eastenders still being popular in the year 2400. It's not surprising that a lot of it seems strange nowadays.

The play's set in Illyria — a far-off, exotic place.
That's why everyone's got funny-sounding names.

People Must've had a Weird Sense of Humour then

A lot's changed since Shakespeare wrote *Twelfth Night* — including people's sense of humour.

1) One thing people used to find particularly rib-tickling was the idea of women dressing up as men. The main character, Viola, pretends to be a boy called Cesario for most of the play.

2) It's funny because everybody else thinks she really is a boy, and they make all sorts of embarrassing mistakes.

3) The play's full of other stupid misunderstandings too. Maria and Sir Toby play a trick on Malvolio, and there's even a jester who goes around cracking silly jokes.

A Hilarious Bun Pun

4) Most of the jokes are puns — words with double meanings. People thought they were hilarious in Shakespeare's time. Tabloid newspapers still use them in headlines.

It's Meant to be Acted — Not Just Read

1) *Twelfth Night* is a play, not a book — it's meant to be seen on a stage with actors playing the parts.

2) When you read it, all you get is what the characters say. It's often pretty hard to follow what's going on.

3) It makes more sense if you imagine what's happening. Think about what the characters are like, and how you think they would speak and act.

Let the words come to life...

4) If you can, watch a TV version of the play. It's a great way to bring it to life — and you're allowed to write about it in your SAT, as long as it fits in with the question.

Dressing up as men — it's a bit of a drag...

This section's all about the things that make the play seem strange to us — and why they're there. You need to understand the things that happen in the play and find out why they happen.

Tricky Play Stuff

This is going to sound really obvious but it's pretty important — a lot of the weird and crazy things about *Twelfth Night* are there just because it's a play.

It's Meant to be Watched by an Audience

The whole point of a play is it tells a story by showing you what happened. You don't just hear the words — you see people talking and fighting. Anybody watching the play is part of the audience.

Unluckily, you only get the words on the page in your SAT — you have to work out what's going on onstage.

The Idea is to Make the Audience Laugh

1) The things that happen and the things people say in the play are there to make the audience feel different moods. Because *Twelfth Night*'s a comedy, most of the things that happen are meant to make the audience laugh.

2) The play isn't just funny. There are other moods the audience could feel too. They could feel sorry for Malvolio at the end of the play.

3) You'll get loads of marks in the SAT if you say what the audience feels about a scene. It sounds tricky but it just means saying what you feel when you read it. Don't forget to give examples from the scene to back up what you're saying.

Don't Confuse Characters with Actors

It's simple enough — characters are the people in the story, like Viola, Olivia and Orsino. The actors are the people who play them. Don't get them confused.

Malvolio is a character. Richard Briers is an actor who played Malvolio.

Sometimes Characters Talk to Themselves

One of the really odd things about *Twelfth Night* is when characters talk to themselves. Don't worry — they haven't suddenly gone barmy.

Viola does it at the end of Act 2, Scene 2. Malvolio does it in Act 2, Scene 5, reading the letter aloud and saying what he thinks about it. In Act 4, Scene 3 Sebastian talks to himself about marrying Olivia.

It's a way for the audience to find out what a character's thinking — the character just says it out loud.

A bit like singing in the shower — you think you're alone, but everyone can hear you...unfortunately.

How the audience feels — with their fingers...

When you write about a scene think what the audience feels as they watch it. Say if it's funny, or makes you feel something else. Learn the difference between the characters and the actors too.

Tricky Play Words

This page deals with those fancy play words that keep coming up. I know they're pretty boring but you really do need to know what they mean. Make sure you learn them all carefully.

Twelfth Night is a Comedy

A comedy is meant to make the audience laugh.

Although things may go wrong in a comedy story, nothing goes seriously wrong.

There's always a happy ending. In Shakespeare's comedies it's usually a wedding.

It's Divided into Acts and Scenes

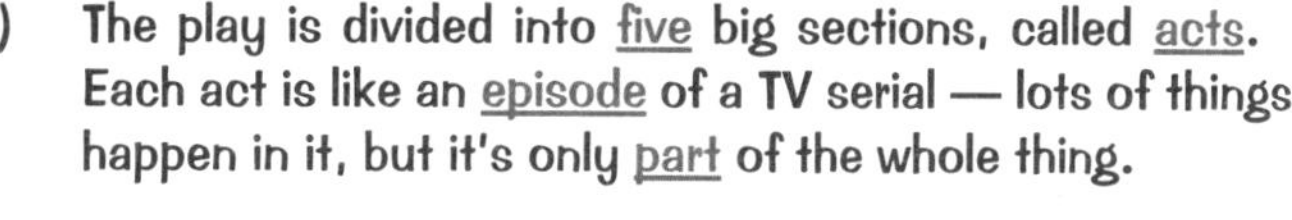

1) The play is divided into five big sections, called acts. Each act is like an episode of a TV serial — lots of things happen in it, but it's only part of the whole thing.

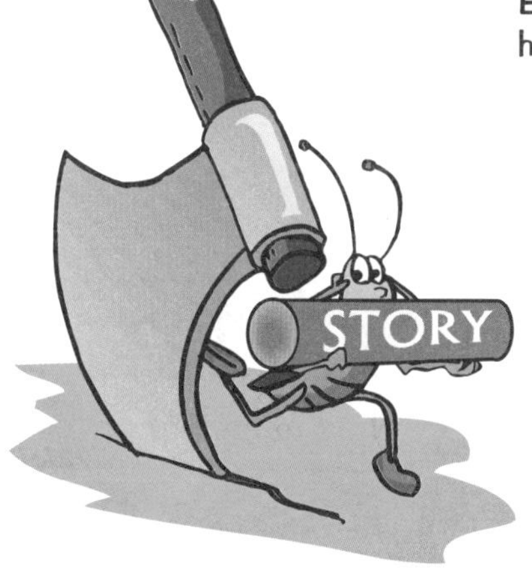

The story gets chopped up with ACTS.

2) Each act is made up of smaller sections called scenes. There's nothing complicated about them. A scene shows you a small bit of the story and then ends. Then a new scene starts that shows you the next bit.

3) Scenes are just a way of breaking up the story. They show that time has passed in the story — one scene could be set in the evening and the next one on the following day.

4) They also let the play move to different places — one scene will happen at Olivia's house, the next one at Duke Orsino's etc.

In your SAT, you'll only have to read one or two scenes from the play.

Stage Directions Say What the Characters are Doing

Stage directions are little phrases in brackets like these.

[*Clock strikes*] [*Draws his dagger*]

These are the really common ones in the play:

Enter = when someone comes onto the stage

Exit = when one person leaves the stage

Exeunt = when more than one person leaves the stage

Aside = to show a character's talking to himself or herself

That act — it was the worst I've ever scene...

You've got to get used to these tricky play words — they come up again and again.

Where the Play's Set

Shakespeare wanted lots of peculiar things to happen in *Twelfth Night* so he set it in Illyria, a place far from England. It helped make the story more believable for his audience.

Illyria is Partly Real and Partly Imaginary

1) Illyria is the area on the Mediterranean where Slovenia, Croatia, Bosnia, and Serbia are today.

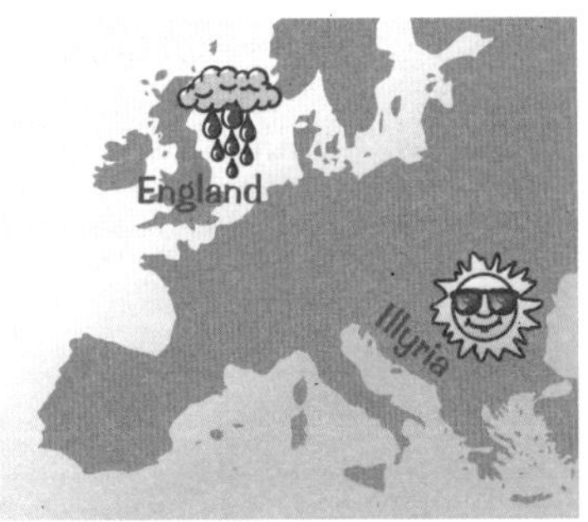

2) At the time Shakespeare was writing the play those places belonged to Venice. A hundred years before, Venice had been one of the richest cities in the world, and it still sounded like a glamorous place.

3) The name Illyria would have made the audience think of a warm, wealthy and beautiful country.

4) The real Illyria was probably quite different from the one in the play. Shakespeare wasn't trying to be realistic — he was trying to describe a place where the audience can believe strange things could happen.

Shakespeare probably never went to the real Illyria. He got his ideas about what it might be like from books.

It's a Very Different Society — With Stricter Rules

When Shakespeare wrote *Twelfth Night* Queen Elizabeth I ruled England. Next came her nobles. Nobles were expected to look after the country and the people in it. In return everyone else was expected to give the nobles obedience and respect.

1) Orsino is the Duke of Illyria. He rules the country like a king. Olivia is a Countess. That makes her a noble too. They are from the most important and powerful level of society.

I'm the king of my castle!

2) Olivia and Orsino's houses are like mini-kingdoms. They are the rulers of their families and servants. Everyone in the household needs to treat them with respect if they want to stay.

3) You were also supposed to respect other people:

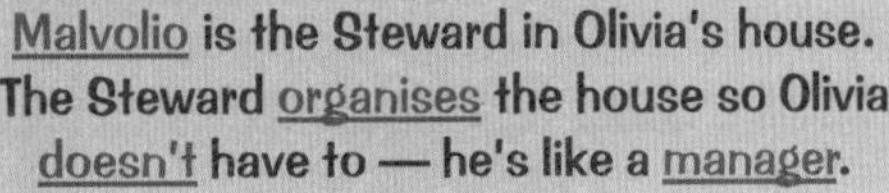
Malvolio is the Steward in Olivia's house. The Steward organises the house so Olivia doesn't have to — he's like a manager.

Viola/Cesario has joined Orsino's household as a courtier. That means she's not a servant, and the servants like Malvolio and Fabian should look up to her.

RSPCR Royal Society for the Prevention of Cruelty to Rulers.

4) The original audience would have been quite shocked at seeing characters behave the way they do in the play. They thought it was dangerous — if people broke the rules, then society could fall apart.

Speak up about the setting — then I'll-'ear ya...

The play's set in an imaginary place — but the rules about how people should behave are from the real world. It's pretty tricky, I know. Get this page learnt and it'll really help you understand the play.

Midwinter Madness

In *Twelfth Night* many of the characters act as if they're temporarily mad. To excuse their odd behaviour, Shakespeare called the play after a festival when everybody behaved in a crazy way.

The Social Rules Get Broken in Twelfth Night

In *Twelfth Night* Shakespeare takes away the normal rules about how people should behave. People act out of character, and do things which don't suit their social position.

1) Taking away the rules like Shakespeare does in *Twelfth Night* is what used to happen at the Feast of Fools. This was a huge midwinter party held every year on 6 January. Another name for 6 January is Twelfth Night, because it is twelve days after Christmas Day.

Tom and Sir Prance-a-lot pick up ideas for their Feast of Fools costumes.

2) At the Feast of Fools servants would dress up as lords and ladies. The nobles could behave in a more silly and undignified way than usual. A 'Lord of Misrule' was chosen to play tricks on the guests.

3) The events in the play don't happen on Twelfth Night, but nearly all the characters behave as though they were at a Feast of Fools party. Everything's all gone crazy.

Love Makes the Characters Act Strangely

Most of the weirdness comes from people falling in love. It makes them do daft things. In those days, people thought love was a kind of madness.

Olivia's love for Cesario makes her lose track of what's going on in her household. In the last scene she even says that she was a bit mad:

> A most extracting frenzy of mine own
> From my remembrance clearly banished his
> Act 5, Scene 1, 270-271

Malvolio and Antonio also do stupid things out of love — Malvolio tries to impress Olivia, and Antonio follows Sebastian to Illyria even though his life's in danger.

Orsino says he's in love with Olivia — for most of the play he mopes around listening to miserable music and moaning about his love like a big jessie.

He's been playing this rubbish for hours now. I want to listen to Britney Spears.

No One's Really Mad — They just Seem Mad

Other characters seem mad because it's the easiest way to explain their odd behaviour.

When Malvolio starts acting weirdly, Olivia thinks he's mad. She lets Sir Toby lock him up as a madman.

> Why, this is very midsummer madness.
> Act 3, Scene 4, 56

Sebastian wonders if Sir Andrew and Sir Toby are mad when they attack him thinking he's Cesario:

> Are all the people mad?
> Act 4, Scene 1, 26

That crazy dentist — he's had an extracting frenzy...

When you write about a scene you've got to say why the characters do what they do, or the examiners won't think you've understood it. Most of the characters act stupidly out of love.

Things Aren't What They Seem

A lot of the funny moments in *Twelfth Night* are when the characters don't really understand what's happening to them. They think one thing, but something else is true — nothing's what it seems.

You Can't Trust The Way Things Look in the Play

But that's not a man, it's a woman, baby!
Oh, behave.

Everybody's acting out of character and on top of that you've got Viola dressed up as a man who looks exactly like Sebastian. It's hardly surprising people get confused — even Feste the jester:

> ...Nothing that is so, is so.
> Act 4, Scene 1, 9

You Can't See the Truth About Anyone Else

People can look like one person and be another. The biggest misunderstanding in the play is over Viola. Everybody except the Captain believes she's a man.

Even objects can be fake — like the letter Malvolio finds which looks like it's been written by Olivia.

Olivia makes a whopping mistake about Viola. She thinks Cesario is wonderful and falls in love — but she doesn't realise Cesario/Viola is actually a woman.

I'm sorry, I thought you were a bloke. But, let's face it, you are a bit mannish.

Antonio gets muddled by Viola too. Viola looks like Sebastian, so Antonio assumes she is Sebastian and gets cross with her for betraying his friendship:

> Will you deny me now?
> Act 3, Scene 4, 323

Antonio and Olivia are judging on appearances — they think that because someone looks beautiful, they're good. But the whole play's about the fact that appearances can be deceiving.

Viola understands that appearances can be misleading:

> nature with a beauteous wall
> Doth oft close in pollution, Act 1, Scene 2, 48-9

"a beauteous wall" = beautiful appearance
"pollution" = evil

A lot of the characters seem to have strong feelings, but those feelings aren't always genuine.

Orsino swears he's in love with Olivia through most of the play. But at the end of the play, he's happy to marry Viola — he knows her much better.

Olivia says she'll mourn her brother for seven years and won't even think about marriage in that time. As soon as she meets Cesario, she changes her mind.

Stitches — they're not what they seam...

When you write about a scene remember to look out for characters misunderstanding who people are and what they're like. It'll show the examiner you really know your *Twelfth Night* onions.

Viola Confuses Everyone

OK, time to own up — there are two really dodgy bits in the story of *Twelfth Night*. One is that Viola dresses up as a man, the other is that she looks exactly like Sebastian.

Viola Pretends to Be a Man

This is one of those things that can seem really odd to us. It's the only way for the story to work — so you've just got to accept it.

1) Don't worry too much about why Viola dresses up as a man. The main reason is that Shakespeare thought it would make his audience laugh. It's a bit like pantomimes — you often get a woman playing the part of the male hero.

2) There's a practical reason for Viola pretending to be a man — it helps her to find a job and a place to live in a country where she's a stranger. It'd be much more difficult and dangerous for a woman on her own.

3) It would have seemed funnier in Shakespeare's time. Women never wore the same clothes as men, and were expected to behave very differently.

Sebastian Doubles the Confusion

Because Viola's dressed like a man, she looks exactly like her brother. She even says she's based her male outfit on her brother:

Everyone else thinks that Sebastian and Viola/Cesario are the same person.

> and he went
> Still in this fashion, colour, ornament,
> For him I imitate.
> Act 3, Scene 4, 358-60

Learn This Bit Now — It Tells You Who Does What

It's seriously confusing — and very unrealistic. Make sure you learn these bits. Sorry, folks, but it's the only way there is to make it less confusing.

Act 3, Scene 4
Antonio rescues Viola/Cesario from the fight with Sir Andrew — but then he gets arrested. Antonio asks for the money he gave Sebastian earlier, but Viola/Cesario doesn't know what he's talking about. Antonio thinks Sebastian has betrayed him.

Act 4, Scene 1
Sir Andrew and Sir Toby try to fight Sebastian, thinking he's Cesario. Olivia comes in and is furious with Toby for fighting Cesario. Olivia takes Sebastian home, and in *Scene 3* they marry. Sebastian thinks she's gorgeous so he goes along with it all, even though he's suspicious — he can't believe his luck.

Act 5, Scene 1
Viola's in big trouble because a lot of people think she's Sebastian.
1) Antonio accuses Viola/Cesario of being an unfaithful friend.
2) Olivia accuses Viola/Cesario of denying being her husband.
3) Orsino accuses Viola/Cesario of betraying him by marrying Olivia.
4) Sir Andrew accuses Viola/Cesario of hurting Sir Toby and him in a fight.

Disguise — well, it's better than dat-guy's...

Everybody falls for Viola's disguise — I told you that comedy doesn't have to be realistic.

Fools

Twelfth Night is full of people making fools of themselves — it's one of the big ideas in the play. There's even a professional Fool. Confusing, I know — so make sure you read this page carefully.

Feste's a Fool — but he's Not Stupid

In many of Shakespeare's plays, kings or rich people have a Fool.
The Fool is paid to be idiotic — he's a professional Clown, paid to make people laugh.
Feste is Olivia's Fool, but he also entertains Orsino.

1) A Fool was allowed to make jokes about anything — Feste even takes the mickey out of Orsino and Olivia. Because he's funny he doesn't have to live by the same rules as everyone else.

> There is no slander in an allowed fool
> though he do nothing but rail
> Act 1, Scene 5, 88-9

2) He's one of the only characters who understands that everything has gone crazy in the play. It seems like everyone else is behaving like a Fool as well. He tells most of the characters this to their faces.

> This fellow is wise enough to play the fool,
> And to do that well craves a kind of wit.
> Act 3, Scene 1, 56-7

3) His jokes are all about wordplay (see page 28) — he twists round what people say to give it another meaning. That takes brains — Viola recognises how clever Feste really is.

4) Feste's a singer as well as a joker. His songs aren't meant to be funny. They're to remind people that love and happiness don't last (page 22).

Perhaps I've gone too far this time.

Fooling Can Also Mean Playing Tricks

Clever practical jokes were part of the Feast of Fools celebrations.
They're part of *Twelfth Night* too.

Maria plants the fake letter for Malvolio to read so as to make a fool of him. She makes him think Olivia is in love with him, and tells him to dress up in a silly costume and act strangely.

Sir Andrew is Just Plain Foolish

Sir Andrew isn't trying to be a fool, although he sometimes tries to be funny.
Foolishness isn't a temporary madness for him, he really is a stupid fool.

...And he asked for two slices of brown toast.
I don't get it. But I'd better laugh anyway or I'll look stupid.

1) Sir Andrew never understands what's going on, and can't keep up with the jokes.

2) Sir Toby is always teasing him — Toby just wants to get money out of him.

3) According to Maria his talents are "most natural". A "natural" was another word for somebody born a bit simple.

When clowns eat too much — they say "No more, I'm fool"...

There are three types of fooling to learn about here — Feste's wordplay, Sir Andrew's natural foolishness, and playing tricks on people. You could be asked about any of them, so learn them.

The End of the Play

At the end of the play the confusion is all cleared up — but it isn't a perfectly happy ending.

Most of the Characters Get What They Deserve

Viola's been loyal to Orsino, and ends up marrying him.

Olivia is married to Sebastian, not Cesario.

Sebastian and Viola are reunited.

Sir Toby and Sir Andrew have been drunk and disorderly and get beaten up by Sebastian.

For most of the play people have been behaving in unexpected ways, but at the end the normal rules come back into force.

Orsino gives up his exaggerated feelings for Olivia, and decides to marry his real friend Viola.

Viola gives up her disguise as a man.

Olivia snaps out of the spell cast by Cesario. She finally sorts out her household — and gets to the bottom of the trick played on Malvolio.

The main characters get married — that's how Shakespeare's comedies always end. Orsino marries Viola, Sebastian marries Olivia and Sir Toby marries Maria.

But Not Everyone Ends Up Happy

At the end of *Twelfth Night* there are a few things which spoil the happy ending.

Malvolio is furious when he finds out he's been tricked. He storms out threatening revenge:

> I'll be revenged on the whole pack of you!
> Act 5, Scene 1, 362

Feste's song at the very end of the play makes him sound sick of fooling. It really feels like the party's over.

You never find out what happens to Antonio.

Oh dear. I seem to have arrived a little early. Could you just stand there, please. The steamroller is on its way.
Are you sure this happens to me? I think you've got the wrong script.

This Play Doesn't Just Make People Laugh

The atmosphere of *Twelfth Night* is very strange. It's meant to be a comedy, but there are lots of sad moments alongside the bits that make you laugh.

All Feste's songs remind you that real life is sad, and happiness is only a passing thing.

The trick played on Malvolio is meant to be fun, but it gets very nasty. Even Sir Toby's sick of it by the end. You start to feel sorry for Malvolio instead of laughing.

A judges' dinner — everyone gets their just desserts...

You could easily get asked about the last scene, so you need to know why it's a happy ending for some characters and a sad ending for others. Watch out for sad bits in other scenes too.

Revision Summary

Twelfth Night is a tricky old play. Don't worry about that complicated Feast of Fools stuff. It's only there to help you understand what happens in the play — you don't have to learn it. Make sure you know all those funny play words — they'll definitely come up. And learn all the stuff about where the play is set and why some of the really odd things in the play happen. They'll come in useful if you get some of the difficult scenes in your SAT. Have a go at these questions now, before you do anything else. They're here for practice, so don't bother cheating. Work through them all without looking back over the section. Then if there's anything you're still not sure about, go back and have another look.

1) Where is the play set?
2) What is the point of a play?
3) What is an audience?
4) How does the play create different moods?
5) What's the difference between characters and actors?
6) Why do people talk to themselves in the play?
7) What is an Act?
8) What is a Scene?
9) What are the stage directions?
10) Why do the characters act strangely in the play?
11) Give two reasons why Viola pretends to be a man.
12) What's Feste's job?
13) Why does Maria play a trick on Malvolio?
14) Who does Sebastian marry? Who does Viola marry?
15) What happens to Malvolio at the end of the play?
16) Give two examples of sad bits in the play.

No, I'm not a viola — I keep telling you...

Why the Language is Hard

Everyone says Shakespeare's plays are brilliant — but they're a nightmare to understand. Or at least they seem that way until you get a few things good and clear in your head.

Watch Out — The Language Looks Really Tricky

1) Shakespeare's language looks hard — but there's no way round it, I'm afraid. You'll be given a scene to read in your SAT — and you've got to be able to understand what happens, or you won't get any marks at all.
2) The best way to work out the language is to read bits from the play out loud with a group of friends. You'll be surprised — stuff that made no sense on the page will actually start to get clearer.
3) Don't forget — it was meant to be spoken out loud. That's the way you're supposed to understand it — don't just sit and read it in your head.

There's no point in worrying about how hard it is — just get on and learn how to read it.

Some of the Play's in Poetry — Some Isn't

Twelfth Night is written in a mixture of poetry and prose — prose is any kind of language that isn't poetry.

Here's how to spot a bit of poetry.

Twelfth Night
Finest Pottery
24-piece Dinner Service

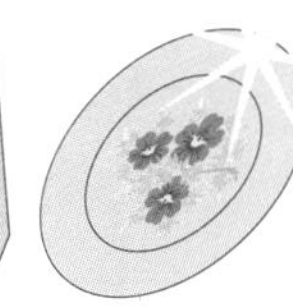

Now, I'm sure I said "poetry"...

Every line starts with a capital letter, even if it comes in the middle of a sentence.

> Your lord does know my mind. I cannot love him.
> Yet I suppose him virtuous, know him noble,
> Act 1, Scene 5, 244-5

Sometimes the last word of a line rhymes with the last word of the next one.

> Then lead the way, good father, and heavens so shine
> That they may fairly note this act of mine!
> Act 4, Scene 3, 34-5

Any bits where the lines run on normally, without extra capitals or rhymes, are in prose.

There's no capital letter.

> Sad, lady? I could be sad. This does make some obstruction in the blood, this cross-gartering, but what of that?
> Act 3, Scene 4, 19-21

I like poetry — I've weighed up the prose and cons...

The secret of this language stuff is just getting used to it. It's never going to get any easier unless you read the play lots. Sounds boring, I know, but it's the only way to work out what's going on.

Old Words and Fancy Words

Well you might think poetry was bad enough — but the play's full of old words and fancy ones too. And when I say old, I mean old...

Here are Some Common Old Words

These words turn up all the time — they make sentences look much harder than they really are.

1) Thou = You Thee = You Thy = Your

The characters use "thou", "thee" and "thy" when they're talking to friends or people they know well:

> Fare thee well.
> Act 3, Scene 4, 198

Olivia is speaking affectionately to Cesario/Viola.

They also use them when they're talking to people of a lower social class.

Orsino calls Cesario/Viola "thou", but she always calls him "you".

Oi, pea-brain, dost thou plan to sit on thy fat lazy backside for ever?
Outrageous! He called me 'thou'! I've never been so insulted!

> What dost thou know?
> Act 2, Scene 4, 105

> But if she cannot love you, sir?
> Act 2, Scene 4, 88

Characters also use them when they're insulting someone.

> If thou thou'st him some thrice, it shall not be amiss.
> Act 3, Scene 2, 43-4

Sir Toby is saying that Sir Andrew should call Cesario "thou" lots in his challenge as an insult.

2) Art = are wilt = will hast = has

Verbs like these go with "thou"

> How now, art thou mad?.
> Act 5, Scene 1, 281

Wow! What a lot of scrolls...

3) Hither = to here

> He shall enlarge him; fetch Malvolio hither.
> Act 5, Scene 1, 267

4) Prithee = I pray thee/I ask you

> Prithee, be content;
> Act 5, Scene 1, 336

5) Hath = has

> He hath not told us of the captain yet.
> Act 5, Scene 1, 365

Watch Out for Fancy Words as well

Shakespeare never uses two words when he can use ten. It can get seriously confusing when he uses loads of fancy-sounding words that really mean something simple and easy.

> He finishèd indeed his mortal act
> That day that made my sister thirteen years.
> Act 5, Scene 1, 236-7

This looks nasty and hard — but here's what it really means.

He died on my sister's thirteenth birthday.

Bless you — two common cold words...

The lingo can get a bit funny sometimes — learning these dusty old words will really help you out.

How to Read the Poetry

It's a pain in the neck, but you've got to know how to read the poetry in the play.

The Poetry Always Has Ten or Eleven Syllables

Every line of poetry in the play has got ten or eleven syllables — or beats.

1 2 3 4 5 6 7 8 9 10
If music be the food of love, play on,

They give the poetry its rhythm.

This is what makes the poetry tricky to read — Shakespeare fiddles with the words to make them fit into lines of ten or eleven syllables with this rhythm.

1. He changes the order of the words to make them fit the line.

> A most extracting frenzy of mine own
> From my remembrance clearly banished his.
> Act 5, Scene 1, 270-71

= a most extracting frenzy of mine clearly banish'd his (frenzy) from my remembrance.

2. Sometimes he makes a word last for an extra syllable.

Normally "fixed" has one syllable — but here you have to say it "fix - ed" so that there are ten syllables in the line.

> And tell them, there thy fixèd foot shall grow
> Till thou have audience.
> Act 1, Scene 4, 17-18

3. Worst of all, he even leaves whole words out — which is a pain.

> He left this ring behind him,
> Would I, or not. Tell him, I'll none of it.
> Act 1, Scene 5,288-9

"Tell him I'll none of it" doesn't seem to make any sense — Shakespeare's left out the word "have" so the line only has ten syllables.

Don't Stop Reading at the End of Each Line

1) Even though each line starts with a capital letter, it doesn't mean it's a separate sentence. Just ignore the capitals and follow the punctuation.

> I hate ingratitude more in a man
> Than lying, vainness, babbling and drunkenness,
> Or any taint of vice whose strong corruption
> Inhabits our frail blood. Act 3, Scene 4, 330-33

There's no full stop so carry on to the next line.

2) There isn't a break in the sentence even when it moves to the next line. You've got to read it as if it's written like this:

> I hate ingratitude more in a man than lying, vainness, babbling and drunkenness, or any taint of vice whose strong corruption inhabits our frail blood.

carrying "on" to the next line...

Making words fit — dieting and exercise...

Every line of poetry in the play has ten or eleven syllables — learn that and the rest'll start to follow.

Different Kinds Of Poetry

I can't say this is the most exciting stuff in the world — but it'll really boost your marks. Some SAT tasks will ask you to talk about how Shakespeare uses language, so it's worth learning.

Most of the Play's in Blank Verse — It Doesn't Rhyme

It's a stupid name, blank verse — all it really means is any bits of poetry that don't rhyme. One key thing that shows they're poetry is the number of syllables in each line — yep, you've guessed it, ten or eleven.

Here's a line of blank verse.

> O then, unfold the passion of my love,
> Act 1, Scene 4, 24

This gets really hairy when two people are talking. Their conversation has to fit into lines of poetry.

This is still poetry, remember.

Things had got really hairy for Bob

ORSINO — Husband?
OLIVIA — Ay, husband. Can he that deny?
ORSINO — Her husband, Sirrah?
MALVOLIO — No, my lord, not I.
Act 5, Scene 1, 138-9

These two bits form one line — that's why they're written like this.

These two bits together make another line.

Some Bits of it Rhyme

Some parts of the play have bits of rhyme in them — especially at the end of scenes. If most of a scene doesn't rhyme but a tiny bit of it does, mention it in your answer.

> Fate, show thy force; ourselves we do not owe.
> What is decreed must be; and this be so.
> Act 1, Scene 5, 297-8

Little tricks like this help your answer no end.

Feste Sings Lots of Songs too

Feste's songs are really important for setting the mood of scenes — that means they're well worth writing about. He sings several sad love songs, and one at the end of the play.

And now the end is near; and so I face the final curtain...

It's all about how life changes as you get older. The last verse finishes off the whole play.

> A great while ago the world begun,
> With hey, ho, the wind and the rain,
> But that's all one, our play is done,
> And we'll strive to please you every day.
> Act 5, Scene 1, 389-end

Shakespeare's verse — blank and you'll miss it...

It isn't just about Shakespeare writing poetry — it's about the kinds of poetry he uses in different scenes. You need to be able to recognise each kind so you can write about them in your SAT.

How to Read the Prose

Prose is anything that isn't written in poetry — it doesn't have to have any rhymes or rhythm. That's the good news. The bad news is it's just as tricky to read.

The Big Problem — Prose has Lots of Long Sentences

Here's the tricky part — all those blinking long sentences. You've got to read them really carefully to make sure you understand what they mean.

Now there's a long winding sentence...

> He will come to her in yellow stockings, and 'tis a colour she abhors, and cross-gartered, a fashion she detests; and he will smile upon her, which will now be so unsuitable to her disposition, being addicted to a melancholy as she is, that it cannot but turn him into a notable contempt.
> Act 2, Scene 5, 193-9

Phew — see what I mean. You'll need to read sentences like this a few times to make sense of them. The secret is to break it up into smaller bits.

He will come to her in yellow stockings,

and 'tis a colour she abhors,

and cross-gartered,

a fashion she detests;

These are the first four bits of the sentence. It's much easier to work out what they mean now.

Malvolio will go to Olivia in yellow stockings and cross-gartered. She hates yellow and she hates cross-gartering.

All the Letters in the Play are in Prose

You need to watch out for letters in the play — there are several important ones.

1. Malvolio finds a fake letter — he thinks it's from Olivia but Maria actually wrote it.

> In my stars I am above thee, but be not afraid of greatness. Some are born great, some achieve greatness, and some have greatness thrust upon 'em.
> Act 2, Scene 5, 135-9

It's written in fancy language to sound posh and grand so that Malvolio believes it's from Olivia.

2. Sir Andrew's challenge to Viola/Cesario is supposed to sound grand and threatening, but it ends up sounding silly instead.

> 'Fare thee well, and God have mercy upon one of our souls! He may have mercy upon mine, but my hope is better, and so look to thyself.'
> Act 3, Scene 4, 152-4

Jolly good luck, old thing. Oh no, you're fighting me, aren't you? Well, in that case, hope you lose, monkey-boy.

What a wally...

3. In the last scene of the play, Malvolio sends a letter to Olivia asking why he's been so badly treated.

> Though you have put me into darkness, and given your drunken cousin rule over me, yet have I the benefit of my senses as well as your ladyship.
> Act 5, Scene 1, 289-91

He uses clear, simple language — it shows Olivia that he isn't mad.

Why the Play's in Poetry and Prose

This is a mega-important bit. You need to learn why some parts of the play are in poetry and the others are in prose. It'll really help you understand what's going on in each scene.

Shakespeare Uses Poetry for Formal or Serious Bits

All the serious bits in *Twelfth Night* tend to be in poetry.

1) Every time Orsino speaks, he uses poetry. It shows he's dead posh and a noble.

> I know thy constellation is right apt
> For this affair. Some four or five attend him
> Act 1, Scene 4, 35-6

2) Viola/Cesario always speaks to Orsino in poetry — their conversations are always really formal.

> VIOLA Sir, shall I to this lady?
> ORSINO Ay that's the theme,
> Act 2, Scene 4, 122

That's what I call paw-tree.

3) All the serious bits about love are in poetry — like all the bits between Olivia and Viola/Cesario, and Olivia and Sebastian.

> OLIVIA Nay, come, I prithee. Would thou'dst be ruled by me!
> SEBASTIAN Madam, I will.
> OLIVIA O, say so, and so be!
> Act 4, Scene 1, 64-65

He Uses Prose for the Comedy Bits

That's one crazy mess...

Everything's a crazy mess in these scenes — nobody's following the rules. That's why the characters speak prose in the comedy scenes. They aren't following the rules for poetry.

1) All the comic characters, like Sir Andrew, Sir Toby and Feste always speak in prose.

2) The scenes about the trick played on Malvolio are all in prose.

3) Viola and Sebastian use prose with Malvolio, Feste, Toby and Andrew.

Anyone in the play who isn't posh speaks prose.

In Some Scenes He uses a Mixture of Both

In Act 1, Scene 5, Viola/Cesario starts off speaking to Olivia in prose, but changes to poetry. Olivia starts in prose too, but also changes to poetry.

Says here that Shakespeare liked to mix it
Er, I don't think they mean, like, with decks and that
CGP

The end of the play is in poetry except for a few speeches. Everything's being sorted out and put back into order — Feste, Sir Toby and Sir Andrew still speak prose; everyone else speaks poetry.

Comedy — there's a business for pro's...

Don't forget — scenes with poetry are formal or serious, scenes with prose are usually comedy bits.

Images In The Play

This play's full of images — some people say they're there to make the language rich and interesting. I think they just make it a lot trickier to follow, myself.

Learn these Three Kinds of Image to Look Out For

Images are just word pictures — they help you see what Shakespeare's describing.

① Similes are when one thing is like something else. They usually use "as or "like"

> as hungry as the sea
> Act 2, Scene 4, 100

> It is as fat and fulsome to mine ear
> As howling after music.
> Act 5, Scene 1, 108-9

They're a kind of comparison — and Shakespeare sticks them in all over the place.

A metaphor is when he says one thing is something else.
Usually it just means using exaggerated language to describe things.

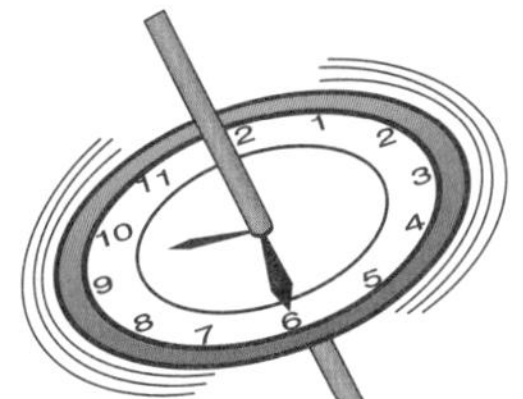

Feste says time is a "whirligig" — a spinning top.
He's basically saying "what goes around, comes around."

> And thus the whirligig of time brings in his revenges.
> Act 5, Scene 1, 360-1

Maria's using a sailing metaphor here to ask Viola/Cesario to leave.

> MARIA Will you hoist sail, sir? Here lies your way.
> VIOLA No, good swabber, I am to hull here a little longer.
> Act 1, Scene 5, 193-4

Lemon Ahoy!

Viola carries it on, calling Maria a "swabber" — a sailor who kept the decks of a ship clean — and saying she is "to hull" there. If a ship was "to hull", it was drifting without hoisting a sail. This isn't just pointless sailor talk — mentioning stuff like this in your exam really helps.

Personification means describing a thing as if it were a person.

> The clock upbraids me with the waste of time.
> Act 3, Scene 1, 126

The clock has just chimed — Olivia says it's criticising her for wasting time, as if it were a person.

Olivia! You are WASTING TIME!
I'm a Shakespeare girl, in a Shakespeare world. I'd like to feel ya, in Illyria...

Simile — doesn't she present Changing Rooms...

Being able to spot different kinds of image — that's what gets you marks, especially if you know the fancy names. Make sure you know exactly what similes, metaphors and personification are all about.

Common Images

Some images turn up time and again all the way through the play — you need to spot them in any scene you read. It's worth it — it'll make a big difference to your marks.

Look for Images Saying Nothing Lasts Forever

Wasting time is one of the big themes of the play — Shakespeare uses lots of different images to say that nothing lasts forever, so people should seize the day.

This song's all about how the future is uncertain, but youth won't last for ever — so people should enjoy love here and now before it's too late.

What is love? 'Tis not hereafter;
Present mirth hath present laughter;
What's to come is still unsure.
In delay there lies no plenty,
Then come kiss me, sweet and twenty;
Youth's a stuff will not endure.
Act 2, Scene 3, 48-53

Come on, babe, you're only young once...

I'm right gorgeous, me.

There are also lots of images of flowers describing beauty — saying it doesn't last long, like a flower.

beauty's a flower
Act 1, Scene 5, 47-8

For women are as roses, whose fair flower,
Being once displayed, doth fall that very hour.
Act 2, Scene 4, 38-9

All these images are about death too — they're saying that once beauty is gone, it's dead forever.

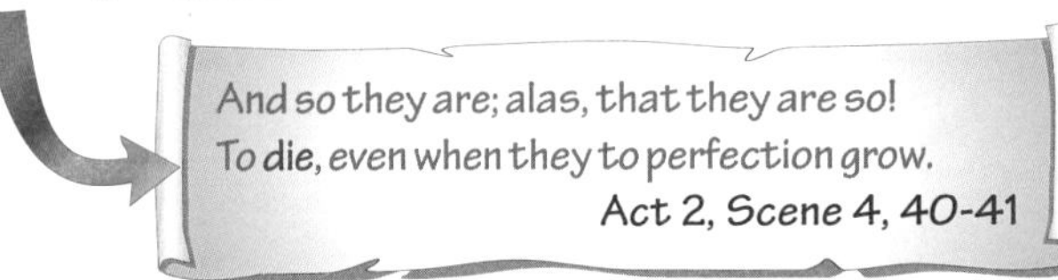
And so they are; alas, that they are so!
To die, even when they to perfection grow.
Act 2, Scene 4, 40-41

Watch For Sea and Jewel Images

The play is all about the effects of a shipwreck, and there are lots of sea images.

From the rude sea's enraged and foamy mouth
Did I redeem. A wrack past hope he was.
Act 5, Scene 1, 72-3

Antonio's talking about rescuing Sebastian from the sea as if Sebastian was a wrecked ship — a "wrack past hope".

There are also several images of precious stones:

thy mind is a very opal.
Act 2, Scene 4, 75

Sea images — they've left me a wreck...

There are loads of different images in the play — this page is about some of the most common ones to watch out for, like anything saying that nothing lasts forever, or anything about the sea or jewels.

Food Images

More important things to learn — this is a kind of image that you'll keep on meeting in the play.

The Play's Stuffed Full of Food Images

Right from the opening line the play uses a food image.

> If music be the food of love, play on,
> Give me excess of it - that, surfeiting,
> The appetite may sicken, and so die.
> Act 1, Scene 1, 1-3

Orsino's saying his love is like an appetite. He wants to feed it with so much music that he'll be full — and won't feel his love any more.

Later on, Orsino talks about love as an appetite again.

He's telling Viola/Cesario that women's love is less strong than men's because it's just an appetite.

What's he talking about,
"Just an appetite"?
FEED ME

> Alas, their love may be called appetite,
> No motion of the liver, but the palate,
> That suffer surfeit, cloyment and revolt,
> But mine is all as hungry as the sea
> And can digest as much.
> Act 2, Scene 4, 98-102

He says his love is as hungry as the sea — it's endlessly hungry.

It's pretty much the opposite of what he said in Act 1 — Shakespeare's making it into a joke by having him use the same image in completely different ways.

When Valentine describes Olivia's grief, he uses a food image too.

> And water once a day her chamber round
> With eye-offending brine; all this to season
> A brother's dead love, which she would keep fresh
> And lasting, in her sad remembrance.
> Act 1, Scene 1, 29-32

Brine is salt water used to keep food fresh. Valentine's saying that Olivia's salt-water tears will keep her dead brother's love fresh in her memory.

Sir Toby uses a food image when he gets cross with Malvolio — "cakes and ale" are an image of fun.

> Art any more than a steward? Dost thou think because
> thou art virtuous there shall be no more cakes and ale?
> Act 2, Scene 3, 113-15

Sir Toby tells Malvolio that just because he's a goody-two-shoes doesn't mean that no one else can have any fun.

If music be the food of love — make mine Meatloaf...

Blimey — there's plenty of food in this play. Keep your eyes peeled for food images in any scene.

Puns and Wordplay

Twelfth Night is supposed to be a comedy — and it's packed full of jokes. Mind you, most of them aren't very funny — they're mostly based on words with two meanings.

Words with Double Meanings are called Puns

Shakespeare loved puns — his plays are full of them. They were really popular at the time he was writing, because everyone thought you were clever if you could make lots of puns.

SIR TOBY I mean, to go, sir, to enter.
VIOLA I will answer you with gait and entrance — but we are prevented.
Act 3, Scene 1, 77-9

Gait, like gate!
Ha ha ha ha ha, I'm so funny!

Sir Toby tells Viola to go and enter, so she makes a pun on the words "gait and entrance" meaning "going and entering", and "gate and entrance".

The Play's Full of this Wordplay

Feste calls himself a "corrupter of words" — part of his job is to find double meanings in words and phrases and make jokes about them.

SIR ANDREW Begin, fool. It begins, "Hold thy peace."
FESTE I shall never begin if I hold my peace.
Act 2, Scene 3, 69-70

Feste makes jokes about the word "fool" in several scenes.
He makes the other characters see that it can mean many different things.

VIOLA Art not thou the Lady Olivia's fool?
FESTE No indeed, sir, the Lady Olivia has no folly. She will keep no fool, sir, till she be married.
Act 3, Scene 1, 28-30

The fool said he'd paid them!

Viola means a professional fool (a jester) — Feste says Olivia won't have a fool until she has a husband. He's saying that all husbands are fools.

Some Double Meanings Cause Misunderstandings

When Malvolio is trying to impress Olivia, he doesn't understand what she's really saying to him.

OLIVIA Wilt thou go to bed, Malvolio?
MALVOLIO To bed? Ay, sweetheart, and I'll come to thee.
Act 3, Scene 4, 28-9

He thinks she wants to sleep with him — in fact she's worried that he's sick.

Wordplay with cakes — all the current puns...

This is the big reason why Shakespeare isn't all that funny to us — his plays are full of wordplay. Be careful with anything Feste says, and watch out for misunderstandings like Act 3, Scene 4.

Revision Summary

Blimey — talk about a tricky business. This language lark is no picnic — Shakespeare uses a lot of old and fancy words... And don't forget all that poetry either. Make sure you've been through this section carefully — it'll help you to spot the different tricks Shakespeare uses in some scenes. So, on to these revision questions. I know they're a pain, but they're the only way you can test what you know. If you get stuck go back and look over the section again. Then have another go. You should be getting the whole lot absolutely right before you move on.

1) What's the best way to work out the language?
2) What does every line of poetry start with?
3) What is prose?
4) What do "thou" and "thee" mean? What does "thy" mean?
5) What does "prithee" mean?
6) How many syllables does every line of poetry have?
7) What three things does Shakespeare sometimes do to make words fit the line?
8) Why shouldn't you stop reading at the end of each line of poetry?
9) What is blank verse?
10) Why are Feste's songs important?
11) What's the big problem with prose?
12) What are the letters in the play written in?
13) When does Shakespeare use poetry in the play?
14) When does he use prose?
15) What are the three kinds of image to look out for?
16) Give three types of common image in the play.

But there are no words in this poem!

Relax, sir, it's only blank verse.

Sid took blank verse a little too far.

Who's Who in the Play

There are loads of characters in the play, with all sorts of tricky names. The main ones are on this page. It's easy to get muddled — so go through this carefully.

Olivia's Household

Sir Andrew Aguecheek
friend of Sir Toby

Sir Toby Belch
a relative of Olivia's living at her house

Olivia
wealthy Countess

Maria
gentlewoman, attendant on Olivia

Fabian
servant

Malvolio
steward — organises house and servants

Feste
Feste officially works for Olivia, but he sometimes works at Orsino's too.

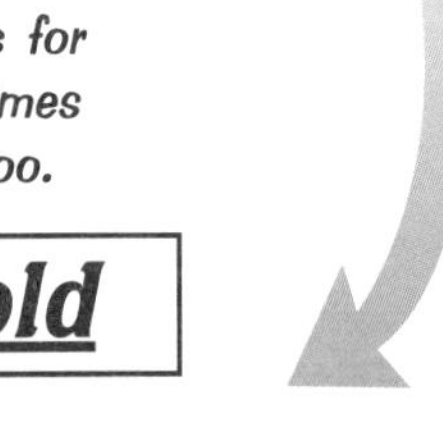

Viola & Sebastian

Viola disguised as **Cesario**

Sebastian
Viola's twin brother

Orsino's Household

Valentine
attendant on Orsino

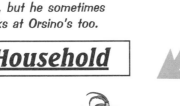

Duke Orsino
ruler of Illyria

Curio
attendant on Orsino

Antonio
friend of Sebastian, rescues him from shipwreck

Olivia and Orsino — they're household names...

Shakespeare didn't half give his characters some funny old names. Use this page to learn the names and who's related to who. It'll make things one heck of a lot easier in the long run.

Orsino

Don't let these funny names put you off — Shakespeare just stuck them in to make the play sound more exotic. The important thing is to learn what sort of people the characters are.

Orsino Rules Illyria

Orsino is a Duke. He's the ruler of Illyria — the chief noble.

In the play, he doesn't do much ruling. He's too busy being in love with Olivia to worry about running the country.

He's rich, he speaks nicely and he's probably handsome. But he's a bit wet too — instead of going to see Olivia himself, he sends other people, right up until the very end of the play.

He's Terribly In Love with Olivia

1) You see Orsino in the first scene of the play. In every scene he's in, he moans about how much he's in love and that it's impossible for him to think about anything else.

Baby, you're irresistible.

2) He never seems to ask himself what Olivia wants — he just assumes he'll win her over in the end.

3) Orsino is sure he's the most in love that anyone's ever been. He's especially sure that his feelings are much deeper than any woman's could be:

> There is no woman's sides
> Can bide the beating of so strong a passion
> As love doth give my heart...
> Act 2, Scene 4, 94-6

4) At the end of the play he finds out he was wrong. The person who loves him most deeply is Viola/Cesario — and she's a woman.

Orsino Snaps Out Of It in the End

Er...I'm not sure you'll like this one.
A surprise? By golly, I love surprises!

At the end of the play Orsino has two big surprises.

The first one's a mistake. He thinks that Cesario has married Olivia behind his back.

The second one is real. He finds out that Cesario's a woman called Viola. He realises that she loves him and has been loyal, and asks her to marry him.

The Duke wins an award — a nobel prize...

If you get asked about Orsino in the SAT, it'll be about love. The thing to remember is that he enjoys the idea of being in love with Olivia, but he doesn't really know what love is till the end of the play.

Viola

You really need to learn what Viola's like — she's the key character in the love story. She falls in love with Orsino and Olivia falls in love with her — it's nice to be popular, I guess.

Viola's New in Illyria

1) Viola and her brother Sebastian are from a town called Messaline.
2) They're on a voyage but they get shipwrecked. Viola ends up in Illyria, thinking that Sebastian has drowned.
3) She has to decide what to do, and how she's going to look after herself in a country where she's a complete stranger.

She Disguises Herself as a Boy to Get a Job

Duke Orsino is somebody Viola's heard her father mention in the past. She decides to dress up as a man, and see if she can get a place serving Orsino.

Don't forget — Viola calls herself Cesario. Be careful not to get confused.

Orsino decides to send her as a messenger to tell Olivia how much he loves her. Unfortunately, Viola soon realises she's fallen in love with Orsino herself:

> Who'er I woo, myself would be his wife.
> Act 1, Scene 4, 42

Viola's Pretty Chilled Out — She Goes with the Flow

When everything starts getting complicated in the play, Viola doesn't hurry to sort things out. She waits to see how things will go, and she doesn't reveal her secret till the end of the play.

When Viola realises Olivia's in love with her, she decides to wait and see what happens. She doesn't tell Olivia she's a woman.

> O time, thou must untangle this, not I,
> It is too hard a knot for me t'untie.
> Act 2, Scene 2, 39-40

Even when Sir Toby is trying to make her fight Sir Andrew, she doesn't give away her secret. Luckily for her, she gets rescued by Antonio.

Dressing up as a boy — breeches the rules a bit...

Viola's a dead important character. You've really got to get to grips with what she's like, and how she deals with her weird situation. Learn the stuff on this page and you'll be well on your way.

Sebastian

Sebastian doesn't appear as often as his sister. But when he does, he really gets things moving. Make sure you know what he's like — if he appears in a scene, there's usually trouble.

Sebastian is Viola's Twin Brother

They look amazingly similar, which is where the problems start.

It's especially confusing because Viola wears clothes just like her brother's.

> ...he went
> Still in this fashion, colour, ornament,
> For him I imitate.
> Act 3, Scene 4, 358-60

For Viola and Sebastian to look so similar they must be quite young. Sebastian can't exactly be a strapping great lad with five o'clock shadow.

Auditioning today for SEBASTIAN

NEXT!!!

He Gets Saved from the Shipwreck

In Act 2 we find out Sebastian was rescued by Antonio.
He stays with Antonio for about three months, before he heads for Orsino's court.

Sebastian thinks Viola drowned in the wreck. He's gutted that he won't see her again:

> She is drowned already, sir, with salt water, though
> I seem to drown her remembrance again with more.
> Act 2, Scene 1, 29-31

He's saying he's drowning her memory with more salt water in his tears.

Sebastian's Got More Get Up and Go than his Sister

1) As soon as Sebastian arrives in town he's eager to go off and see the sights.

2) When Sir Andrew and Sir Toby attack him in Act 4, Scene 1, he's happy to fight back.

3) When Olivia invites him to her house, he goes with her.

4) He realises it's a weird situation, but he really fancies Olivia, so he's happy to go along with it even though he thinks it's crazy:

> ...I am mad,
> Or else the lady's mad...
> Act 4, Scene 3, 15-16

5) In Act 5, Scene 1, Sebastian apologises to Olivia for beating up Sir Toby and Sir Andrew. They were both drunk, but it's still quite impressive to win a fight against two grown men.

Maggot twins — they always go round in pears...

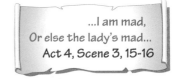

Sebastian only gets important in Act 4, where everyone starts mistaking him for Viola/Cesario. You need to know how different he is from Viola — he's happy to fight and he loves Olivia...She doesn't.

Olivia

Olivia's the object of Orsino's love — but she falls for Viola/Cesario.
She starts off as a sad figure, but ends up looking pretty silly.

Olivia's a Beautiful Countess

My dear brother, for seven years shall I wear this veil of mourning.

1) Olivia lives in the same town as Orsino. She's a Countess so she's part of the same social circle as Duke Orsino.
2) Olivia's father and brother have died recently. She's the heir to the family house and money.
3) When her brother died Olivia swore to shut herself away from the world. She is so sad that she plans to wear a veil and stay in her house for seven years, grieving for her brother.

She's a Powerful Person

Olivia's in charge of her household — even her uncle Sir Toby Belch.
She has to keep everyone in order, calmly and fairly.

Honestly, you two. When are you going to grow up?
He's picking on me.

In Act 1, Scene 5, Feste and Malvolio start bickering. Malvolio insults Feste's fooling, and Olivia has to break up the argument. She tells Malvolio exactly what she thinks of his attitude:

> Oh, you are sick of self-love Malvolio...
> Act 1, Scene 5, 85

Later in the same scene she tells Feste to behave himself too:

> Now you see, sir, how your fooling grows old, and people dislike it.
> Act 1, Scene 5, 105-6

When She Falls in Love She Falls Apart

Olivia falls in love with Viola/Cesario almost as soon as she sees him.
She forgets everything else immediately.

I always go to pieces when I fancy someone.

It's as if she's gone mad — all she cares about is seeing Viola/Cesario again.
To the audience, she's making a fool of herself because Viola/Cesario is really a girl.

She loses track of what's going on in her household. She doesn't realise Malvolio's been tricked in Act 3 Scene 4 — she thinks he's gone mad and lets Toby deal with the problem, and it all gets out of hand.

She marries Sebastian thinking he's Cesario — she only discovers her mistake at the end of the play.

The round table — that was a social circle...

Olivia's a sad and serious figure at the start of the play, but she ends up looking daft because she falls in love with a girl. Remember — the trick on Malvolio only works because she's distracted.

Malvolio

Malvolio's a weird character — in the early part of the play you want to hate him, and it's funny watching him fall for Maria's trick. But by the end of the play you can't help feeling sorry for him.

Malvolio is Olivia's Steward

1) His job is to manage Olivia's house. He's her chief servant — a responsible job.

2) Malvolio takes his job really seriously, and he's always telling people what to do. The way he does it is really annoying though — he's got no sense of humour and he's very rude and bossy.

3) Everyone apart from Olivia hates Malvolio. In Act 1, Scene 5, he insults Feste's fooling:

> I marvel your ladyship takes delight in such a barren rascal.
> Act 1, Scene 5, 78-9

4) In Act 2, Scene 3, Malvolio storms in when Feste, Sir Toby and Sir Andrew are drinking and singing late at night, disturbing everyone. He insults them and threatens to tell Olivia that Maria gave them wine.

> My masters, are you mad?
> Act 2, Scene 3, 87

> She shall know of it, by this hand.
> Act 2, Scene 3, 122-3

HOUSE RULES
no dancing
no singing
no shouting
no drinking
NO FUN

Maria Tricks Him in Revenge

She writes a love-letter to Malvolio that looks like it comes from Olivia. It tells Malvolio to do all sorts of stupid things to prove his love for her.

Even better, Malvolio is so arrogant that he already thinks that Olivia fancies him. When he finds the letter, he's convinced Olivia loves him madly:

> for every reason excites to this, that my lady loves me.
> Act 2, Scene 5, 160-61

At the End You Start Feeling Sorry For Him

1) In Act 3, Scene 4, Malvolio appears in front of Olivia with a big smile and a silly outfit, and it's still very funny. Unfortunately, Olivia thinks he really is mad. She says Sir Toby should look after him. This is where the story takes a nasty turn.

2) Sir Toby and Maria lock him up as though he really is mad. They keep him away from Olivia so he's got no chance to defend himself. They send Feste to him pretending to be a priest — just to make fun of him even more.

3) Even Sir Toby realises the joke's gone too far, but he doesn't know what he can do about it. When Malvolio finally gets out, he's furious with Olivia. After he finds out about the trick, he rushes off promising revenge on everyone.

It's a really unpleasant ending for the comedy story.

Malvolio — sounds like a sick Italian rodent...

Malvolio's one of the hardest characters to write about. You need to be careful to look at which scene you're given — in the early scenes he's really horrible but by the end you feel sorry for him.

Sir Toby and Sir Andrew

These two start off as the comic relief in the play — but they end up getting their just desserts for all the trouble they cause.

Sir Toby Belch is a Self-Centred Sponger

He's Olivia's uncle — but he's living in her house because he has no money of his own. He's also sponging money off Sir Andrew, by telling him that Olivia will marry him.

1) Even though he lives in Olivia's house, he refuses to live by her rules:

> I'll confine myself no finer than I am.
> Act 1, Scene 3, 9

2) He thinks Olivia's being stupid to mourn her brother's death.

> What a plague means my niece to take the death of her brother thus?
> Act 1, Scene 3, 1-2

3) As if that wasn't bad enough, he spends almost all of the play drunk.

4) Sir Toby hates Malvolio and enjoys the trick played on him. He takes the mickey out of Sir Andrew all the time and forces him to challenge Viola/Cesario to a duel just for a laugh.

5) At the end of the play we're told he's married Maria. The last time he comes on stage is after he and Andrew have been beaten up by Sebastian. He's not a funny character any more, and he turns on Andrew and tells him exactly what he really thinks of him.

> Will you help? — an ass-head and a coxcomb and a knave, a thin-faced knave, a gull!
> Act 5, Scene 1, 195-6

Sir Toby and Sir Andrew are definitely not heroic, even though they're knights.

Sir Andrew Aguecheek Just Doesn't Get It

1) Sir Andrew's a bit thick — he doesn't really know what's going on. He tries to join in with Sir Toby and Feste's witty jokes, but he can't quite manage it.

2) Sir Toby is only friends with him because of his money, and so that he can laugh at him — Andrew doesn't stand a chance with Olivia but he doesn't realise it.

3) Sir Andrew is cowardly but very funny. Even though he's silly, there's a moment when you realise that deep down he might be decent, if only Sir Toby weren't controlling him:

> I was adored once too.
> Act 2, Scene 3, 181

He's a sad figure as well — none of his friends are real. They're only using him.

An evening with Sir Toby — a good knight out...

Sir Toby is a brilliant character. The examiners love to set tasks that ask you to write as if you are Sir Toby. You've got to know what makes him tick — other people's money, wine and laughter.

Feste

Almost everything Feste says is a joke, or a play on words. He's not really a character in his own right — he's more of a commentator on what happens.

It's Feste's Job to Make People Laugh

1) Feste's a professional Fool or Clown. It's his job to entertain people by joking and singing.

2) He's allowed to make jokes about anything he wants to — even if it's dead offensive.

> There is no slander in an allowed fool
> Act 1, Scene 5, 88-9

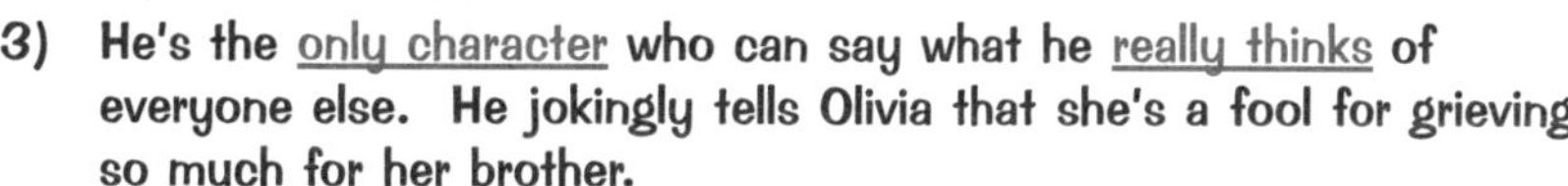

3) He's the only character who can say what he really thinks of everyone else. He jokingly tells Olivia that she's a fool for grieving so much for her brother.

> Good madonna, give me leave to prove you a fool.
> Act 1, Scene 5, 53-4

His jokes are based on puns and wordplay — see page 28.

He's in it for the Money

Feste's supposed to be Olivia's Fool, but he's happy to go wherever the money is.

He sings sad songs for Orsino when the Duke's feeling melancholy, but he also sings sad love songs for Sir Toby and Sir Andrew when they're drunk.

He jokes with people to make money too — with Viola/Cesario in Act 3, Scene 1; with Sebastian in Act 4, Scene 1; and with Orsino in Act 5, Scene 1.

The only time Feste isn't worried about money is when he pretends to be a priest for the trick on Malvolio.

Feste Really Hates Malvolio

Feste is livid at what Malvolio says about him in Act 1, Scene 5. It's a really harsh criticism of his skills.

At the end of the play, Feste tells Malvolio he was involved in the trick, and almost quotes what Malvolio said to him (see page 35).

> But do you remember - 'Madam, why laugh you at such a barren rascal, and you smile not, he's gagged'?
> Act 5, Scene 1, 358-360

Feste only got involved in the trick to get his revenge on Malvolio.

Melon-collie — is that a fruity kind of dog...

Feste's an odd character — you never really get to know him. He's only important in the way that he relates to the other characters in the play. Remember — his job is to make jokes and entertain.

Maria and Fabian

Blimey — these characters keep on coming. Maria and Fabian are important for the Malvolio story.

Maria's the Brains Behind the Trick on Malvolio

Maria is Olivia's gentlewoman — her personal attendant.

Maria's good friends with Sir Toby. In Act 1, Scene 3, she warns him that Olivia isn't happy with his behaviour, and tells him that Sir Andrew is a worthless fool.

In Act 1, Scene 5, she warns Feste that Olivia's cross with him for disappearing. He's sharp enough to spot that she and Sir Toby should get together.

> ...if Sir Toby would leave drinking, thou wert as witty a piece of Eve's flesh as any in Illyria.
> Act 1, Scene 5, 24-6

She's furious with Malvolio when he tells her off for giving Toby and Andrew wine in Act 2, Scene 3 — but because he's the chief servant, she can't answer him back. That's when she decides to get her revenge by writing the fake love letter.

Maria doesn't appear in the last scene of the play, but Fabian says that Sir Toby has married her.

Fabian Works for Olivia too

Fabian is another member of Olivia's household.
He's got a grudge against Malvolio too so he joins in with the trick.

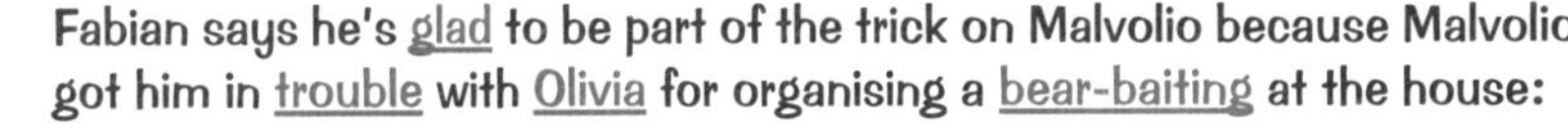

1) Fabian says he's glad to be part of the trick on Malvolio because Malvolio got him in trouble with Olivia for organising a bear-baiting at the house:

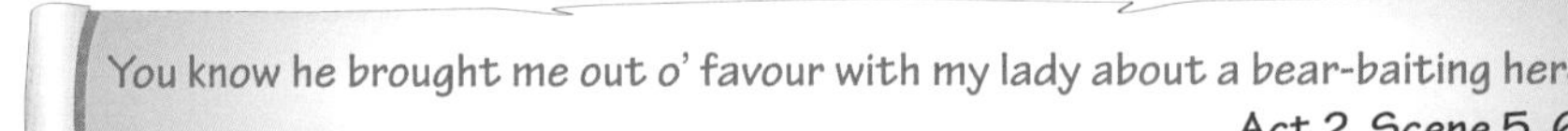

> You know he brought me out o' favour with my lady about a bear-baiting here.
> Act 2, Scene 5, 6-8

2) He also helps Sir Toby wind up Sir Andrew and Viola/Cesario before their duel.

3) In the last scene, he's a lot more serious — when Olivia offers to let Malvolio investigate who played the trick, Fabian confesses everything.

4) He says it was Toby and he who planned it — but actually Maria did. He tries to say it was all just a joke, but that there were good reasons for it on both sides.

> How with a sportful malice it was followed
> May rather pluck on laughter than revenge,
> Act 5, Scene 1, 350-51

Fabian has a grudge — sounds painful...

Fabian and Maria aren't in many scenes, but that doesn't mean you can ignore them. If you get any of the scenes about the trick they'll be there, so you'll need to know why they hate Malvolio.

Antonio and Others

Here's the last lot of characters to get to know, so get stuck in.

Antonio is Sebastian's Friend

Antonio's a sea-captain, and Sebastian's friend.

1) Antonio rescues Sebastian from the shipwreck. Sebastian stays with him for three months afterwards and they become good friends.

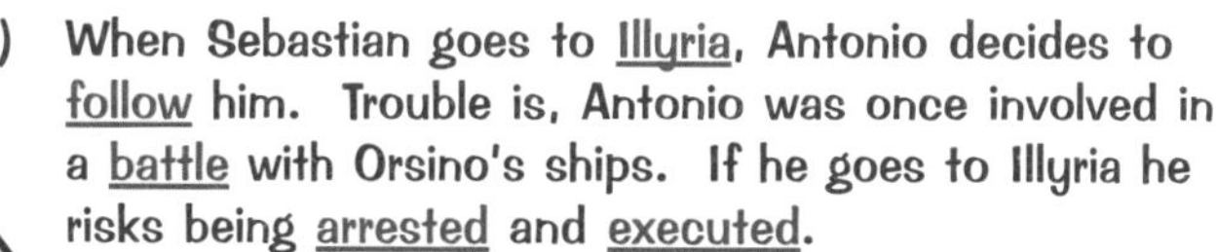

2) When Sebastian goes to Illyria, Antonio decides to follow him. Trouble is, Antonio was once involved in a battle with Orsino's ships. If he goes to Illyria he risks being arrested and executed.

3) When they meet in Illyria, Antonio gives Sebastian his purse and goes to find an inn to stay hidden. Later he goes to look for Sebastian and comes across Viola/Cesario fighting Sir Andrew.

4) He rescues her, thinking it's Sebastian, but he's arrested by the police. He asks for his purse and doesn't get it — he thinks Sebastian's betrayed him.

5) In Act 5, Scene 1, Antonio tells Orsino his story but no one believes him — it's only when Sebastian comes in that he's recognised. But even at the end of the play it's not clear whether he'll be let off or locked away.

Antonio's a bit of an old seadog...

The Other Characters Are Nothing to Worry About

There are a few other minor characters in the play.
You don't need to know much about them, just remember who they are.

1) The Captain of the wrecked ship is from Illyria.

He's with Viola when she washes up on the shore, and helps her get to Orsino's court, and disguise herself as a man.

He's just another old seadog...

2) Curio and Valentine are attendants of Orsino. They don't get involved in the main story much.

3) There's a Priest who marries Olivia to Sebastian.

4) The two officers who arrest Antonio don't have time to show a personality. They just do their job then shuffle off.

On stage you could have extras too — lords at Orsino's court, or sailors on the shore with Viola and the Captain. That would be up to the director though. You don't need them for the story to make sense.

Minor characters — I really dig them...

Good news — you don't need to know as much about these characters as about, say, Viola or Malvolio. Just make sure you know who they are, in case they turn up in the scene you get for your SAT.

Revision Summary

If you don't know who's who in the play it can get seriously confusing. You need to know the names of all the main characters — and how to spell them. What's more you've got to know what they're like, and the main events they get involved in. Keep going through these questions until you can answer them all without cheating. Answer them all, I said.

1) Who rules Illyria?
2) Who is he in love with?
3) What two surprises does he get at the end of the play?
4) Why does Viola dress up as a man?
5) What's Viola like? Does she: *a) Mope around making everyone's life a misery?*
   b) Try to sort everyone's problems out?
   c) Leave things to sort themselves out?
6) Whose brother is Sebastian?
7) What does he think happened to his sister?
8) Who saves Sebastian from the shipwreck?
9) Which two characters does Sebastian beat up?
10) Why is Olivia in mourning at the start of the play?
11) How does Olivia usually deal with things? *a) calmly and fairly* *b) like a gibbering wreck* *c) as if she doesn't care*
12) Who does Olivia fall in love with?
13) How does she behave when she's in love?
14) What's Malvolio's job?
15) Why does everyone find him so annoying? *a) He steals money from Olivia.* *b) He doesn't approve of anyone having fun.* *c) He sings really badly and out of tune.*
16) Whose idea is it to play a trick on Malvolio?
17) What relation is Sir Toby to Olivia?
18) Who's the thick one out of Sir Andrew and Sir Toby?
19) What's Feste's job?
20) Why does he work at Orsino's house too?
21) Why does Antonio get arrested?
22) Why does he ask Viola/Cesario for a purse?

Sadly, the National Rodent Theatre didn't realise that there isn't a 12th Knight in the play.

What Happens in Act One

Act 1 Scenes 1 & 2

You have to write about one scene in the test and it could be any scene. This section tells the story of the play — showing what every scene's about. Use it to learn the whole story.

Scene One — The Duke's Madly in Love

This scene is nice and short, but it's a really strange opening for a play. This drippy fellow starts telling us all about love — straightaway we know what the play's all about.

1 Orsino is in love
Orsino talks about his love. He asks for more music to help him enjoy it, and then suddenly changes his mind. He can't concentrate on anything. lines 1-15

2 Curio invites him to go and hunt
Curio is just trying to distract Orsino, but the Duke turns his words into an image of his love for Olivia. lines 16-22

3 Valentine comes in with a message from Olivia
Orsino had sent Valentine to tell Olivia about his love, but Valentine didn't get in to see her. Her maid told him that Olivia's still mourning the death of her brother. lines 23-32

4 Orsino imagines Olivia falling in love with him
He compares the love she feels for her brother to the love she might one day feel for him, and imagines he will be king of her heart. lines 33-41

Duke Orsino has got it bad. Everything around him reminds him of his love — the music, the invitation to go hunting, even Olivia's grief for her dead brother.

Scene Two — Viola's been Shipwrecked near Illyria

Sebastian.
Seb's dead, already.
Nah, I doubt it. I reckon he'll turn up later on.

Viola doesn't worry about the future — she thinks it'll all work out fine.

> What else may hap, to time I will commit. (60)

She says something similar at the end of Act 2, Scene 2.

1 Viola, the Captain and his sailors arrive in Illyria
Viola is worried that her brother might have drowned. The Captain says that he saw Viola's brother hanging on to a piece of wood floating in the water. lines 1-20

2 The Captain knows the area and all the gossip
It turns out that the Captain was brought up nearby, and he tells Viola that Duke Orsino rules the area. He also tells her about Orsino's love for Olivia. Viola says she understands why Olivia's shut herself away. lines 21-46

3 Viola decides to disguise herself as a boy
Viola asks the Captain to help her become a servant of the Duke. She believes that everything will sort itself out in time. lines 47-64

Viola's like the dishes — she's all washed up...

These scenes are both short and slightly boring. In the first scene all you see is Orsino banging on about how in love he is. Mind you, both scenes give you quite a bit of information — Olivia's brother's dead, and Viola's brother might be drowned. It's all useful, so get on and learn it.

Act 1
Scenes 3 & 4

What Happens in Act One

It's no good rushing this section. In fact that's a truly terrible idea. You could get any scene in the exam. Recognising where a scene comes in the story will be a huge help in the test.

Scene Three — Sir Toby and Maria Tease Sir Andrew

At last — here's a nice jolly scene to make a change from the last two.

The real reason Sir Toby is friends with Sir Andrew is because he has money:

> Why, he has three thousand ducats a year. (20)

Everything else Sir Toby says about him here is a joke.

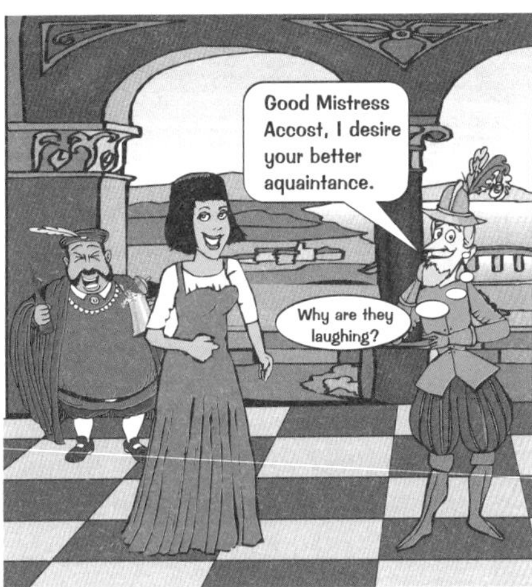

Good Mistress Accost, I desire your better aquaintance.
Why are they laughing?

1 Maria tells Sir Toby that Olivia is cross with him
Maria warns Sir Toby about his late nights and drunkenness. She tells him to be careful. Sir Toby refuses and makes a joke of it. lines 1-12

2 Maria and Sir Toby argue about Sir Andrew
Maria warns Sir Toby that Olivia's also angry about him spending so much time with Sir Andrew. Maria says Andrew is a money-waster, an idiot, a drunk and a coward. Sir Toby jokingly praises Andrew's gifts at music and foreign languages. lines 13-40

3 Sir Andrew comes in
Sir Toby and Maria make fun of Sir Andrew. He doesn't understand their jokes. Maria leaves. lines 41-74

4 Sir Andrew and Sir Toby have a chat
Sir Andrew is miserable. He says he plans to go home. Sir Toby changes his mind and convinces him not to give up on Olivia. Sir Andrew decides to stay and they start making lots of jokes. lines 75-131

Scene Four — Viola's Made a Big Hit with Orsino

This is the first time we see Viola dressed as a boy.

1 Viola has become Orsino's favourite
Viola is dressed as a boy and calls herself Cesario. The Duke is already fond of Cesario. lines 1-8

2 The Duke sends Cesario to Olivia on his behalf
Orsino has told Viola/Cesario all his secrets. Now he sends Cesario to Olivia to tell Olivia that he loves her. lines 9-25

3 Orsino thinks Olivia will listen to Cesario
He thinks Olivia will be more likely to listen to a youth. He says that Cesario looks and sounds more like a woman than a man, so Olivia will listen. lines 26-40

4 Viola is in love with the Duke
She'll go and talk to Olivia, but at the end of the scene she tells us she's really in love with the Duke herself. lines 40-42

Blimey — three days have already gone by since Scene 2:

Dude looks like a lady.

> He hath known you but three days, and already you are no stranger. (2-4)

This bit's a joke — Orsino doesn't know that Cesario really is a girl, but the audience does. Shakespeare's having a laugh.

Isn't that a Bond film — Orsino Royale...

Don't get muddled — you need to know the order things happen in and where they're happening.

What Happens in Act One

Act 1 Scene 5

Here's where the play starts to get really interesting — Olivia meets Viola/Cesario and falls in love.

Scene Five — Viola/Cesario turns up at Olivia's House

First of all you get to see the other two main comedy characters in action — Feste and Malvolio.

1 Feste's in trouble with Olivia
He's been skiving somewhere — and Maria warns him that Olivia's on the warpath. She tells him she won't make any excuses for him — Olivia may well throw him out. lines 1-33

It looks like Feste's been gone for a while. He has to impress Olivia to get his job back.

2 He's got to make Olivia laugh — or else
Olivia and Malvolio appear. She asks for Feste to be taken away. He starts cracking jokes to show off his wit. Olivia is quite amused, and tells Malvolio off for being rude to Feste. lines 34-93

3 Maria says there's a young man at the gate
Maria says someone's at the gate. Olivia tells Malvolio to send him away if he comes from the Duke. Olivia warns Feste not to fool too much. lines 94-109

4 Sir Toby arrives home drunk (again)
Olivia asks him who's at the gate. Toby's too drunk to say. lines 110-132

5 Malvolio comes back with news
The young man at the gate's determined to speak to Olivia. She is curious and decides to speak to him, but puts her veil on first. lines 133-159

Viola/Cesario speaks very sweetly to Olivia. She wants to do her job well to please Orsino.

6 It's not really a man, it's Viola/Cesario
Viola/Cesario comes in and speaks to Olivia. Olivia is enchanted by Cesario, and sends her attendants away. Olivia takes off her veil, and Cesario sees her face. Viola/Cesario tells Olivia how in love the Duke is, but Olivia's only interested in Cesario. lines 160-267

7 Uh oh — Olivia's falling in love
Olivia wants Cesario to come again. She offers him money, but Viola/Cesario refuses and leaves. Olivia's very impressed with Cesario's looks and actions, and realises she's falling in love with him. lines 267-286

8 Olivia sends Malvolio after Cesario
Olivia calls Malvolio and gives him a ring to take to Cesario. She tells Malvolio that Cesario left it, and she wants to return it. Malvolio takes the ring. lines 286-298

Olivia's lying — she just wants to give Cesario a present so that he'll visit her again soon.

Feste and the twins — I hate all this cloning around...

This Viola/Cesario business is confusing. Just remember — everyone thinks she's a boy. Olivia doesn't know she's fallen in love with a woman dressed as a man, but the audience does. It's all a big joke.

Act 2 Scenes 1 & 2

What Happens in Act Two

OK, this is where you meet twin number two, Sebastian. Now it starts to get really confusing.

Scene One — Here's Viola's brother, Sebastian

Sebastian's been saved too — that's a good start.

1 Sebastian was rescued by Antonio
Sebastian's been with Antonio a while, but now he wants to move on. Antonio offers to go with him, but Sebastian's still sad. He would rather travel alone. lines 1-14

2 Sebastian thinks Viola is dead
Sebastian explains that he has a twin sister who was drowned in the shipwreck, and he's really upset. lines 15-37

3 He's heading for Orsino's court
He says goodbye to Antonio. He says he's almost ready to cry, and leaves. Antonio tells the audience he has enemies in Orsino's court, so he shouldn't follow Sebastian, but he will anyway. lines 38-47

My poor sister! Ah, Viola!
See, I told you. Sebastian's alright. He's been rescued by another ship.
You've seen this play before, haven't you?

Scene Two — Things Get More Difficult for Viola

Now it's all starting to become clear to Viola — she's in a real pickle.
She loves Orsino, Orsino loves Olivia, and Olivia loves...her. Oops.

Malvolio speaks to Viola/Cesario coldly and rather rudely.

Duke Orsino loves Olivia.
The duke is attracted to Viola, but thinks she's a man.
Olivia loves Cesario.
Cesario (Viola) loves the duke.
Oh dear. I'm really making a mess here.

Viola doesn't do anything about the problem. She's going to leave it to sort itself out.

1 Malvolio gives the ring to Cesario
Malvolio catches up with Viola/Cesario and delivers the message from Olivia. He throws the ring down on the ground. lines 1-15

2 Viola's left scratching her head
Viola didn't leave a ring with Olivia. She suspects Olivia has fallen in love with her as a boy, and realises her disguise has worked too well. She says to herself it's easy for a woman to fall in love with the wrong man because women are weak. lines 16-31

3 Only time'll sort out this mess
Orsino loves Olivia but he doesn't stand a chance, Viola loves Orsino but she doesn't stand a chance, and Olivia loves Cesario — and she really doesn't have a chance. It's too tricky for Viola to solve. lines 32-40

Playing Viola — a job for a musician perhaps...

These two scenes are dead important — it's the first time we see Sebastian. Antonio's decision to follow him is crucial for later, so don't forget it. It's also where Viola realises the mess she's in.

What Happens in Act Two

Act 2 Scene 3

It's party time in this scene. Toby's drunk — in fact he's slaughtered — and so's Sir Andrew. They decide to have a sing-song, but you can bet Malvolio isn't amused.

Scene Three — Malvolio has a barney with Sir Toby

1 Andrew and Toby are chatting drunkenly
Sir Toby makes lots of jokes that Andrew doesn't get. They both demand more wine. lines 1-14

2 Feste comes to join the fun
Sir Andrew and Sir Toby ask him for a song. He jokes with them until they pay him. He sings two love songs, then they all sing together. lines 15-72

3 Maria's had enough of their racket
She warns them to keep the noise down, in case Olivia calls Malvolio to come down and throw them out. They carry on singing. lines 73-86

4 Malvolio tries to break up the party
He storms in and shouts at them. He threatens to have Sir Toby kicked out. lines 87-101

5 The lads carry on singing anyway
Sir Toby tells Malvolio that just because he's a goody-goody, it shouldn't mean that anyone else should be denied their fun. lines 102-119

6 Malvolio storms off in huff
Malvolio says he's telling on Maria to Olivia. Maria's not impressed. lines 120-123

Feste isn't drunk — he's there to make money out of them, and joins the fun for a laugh.

I'm going to tell on you.
I get knocked down, but I get up again. You're never gonna...
I luv you, youuu're my besht mate....

If I do not gull him into a nayword, and make him a common recreation, do not think I have wit enough to lie straight in my bed: I know I can do it. (135-8)

Maria can't answer Malvolio back to his face in case she ends up in trouble with Olivia — she has to be more sneaky to get her revenge.

7 Maria's got a plan for revenge
Sir Andrew and Sir Toby want to challenge Malvolio to a duel, but Maria's got an idea for making a complete fool of him. lines 124-138

8 Maria describes Malvolio's faults
He's pompous. He thinks he's the bees knees, and thinks anyone who looks at him will love him. lines 139-153

9 Here's Maria's cunning plan
She'll write a love letter to Malvolio in Olivia's handwriting. He'll think Olivia's in love with him. It's an ace plan. Maria leaves. lines 154-176

10 Sir Toby and Sir Andrew stay up longer
Sir Toby talks about how great Maria is, and tells Andrew to send for more money. They decide to stay up and have another drink. lines 177-191

A family of Scottish jokers — a punning clan...

Right — this is where the seeds of the trick are sown. Everyone is seriously narked with Malvolio by the end of this scene. He's spoiled the party and threatened to tell Olivia — now it's revenge time.

Act 2 Scene 4

What Happens in Act Two

The tension between Viola/Cesario and Orsino is building up now. Viola is in love with Orsino, and it's starting to show. If only he knew Cesario was really a woman...

Scene Four — Orsino and Cesario Talk about Love

Orsino doesn't mention Olivia until later in the scene — he's just enjoying being in love.

1 Orsino asks to hear a song
Curio says that Feste sang the song, and he's not here. Orsino sends Curio off to look for him. lines 1-14

2 Orsino tells Cesario about love
He tells Viola/Cesario to remember him and his odd behaviour if he ever falls in love. lines 15-20

3 He asks for Viola/Cesario's opinion
Orsino thinks Viola/Cesario knows about love. He asks who Viola/Cesario is in love with. lines 21-5

4 It sounds surprisingly familiar...
Viola/Cesario describes the woman as being like the Duke. Orsino thinks she must be too old. lines 25-41

This bit can be really funny. Viola's talking about Orsino, but he doesn't realise it. The audience does — which makes it comical.

5 In comes Feste to sing his song
Feste sings that being in love is like dying, and gets paid. He thinks Orsino's being self-indulgent. lines 42-78

6 Orsino sends Feste and Curio away
Orsino tells Viola/Cesario to go to Olivia again. Viola/Cesario tries to explain that Olivia doesn't love Orsino. He doesn't believe it. lines 79-93

7 They talk about love
Orsino says that men's love is stronger than women's love. Viola/Cesario tells Orsino that women can feel just as strongly as men. She gives the example of a sister — but she's really talking about her own feelings for Orsino. lines 94-125

The song breaks up the tension between Orsino and Cesario.

ORSINO But died thy sister of her love, my boy?
VIOLA I am all the daughters of my fathers house,
And all the brothers too: and yet I know not.
(120-2)

The state of British tennis — let's talk about love...

Viola can't hide the fact that she's in love with Orsino, try as she might. It's a good job he's so wrapped up in himself. Remember — he doesn't know she's really a girl, he thinks she's a boy.

What Happens in Act Two

Act 2 Scene 5

This scene's one of the funniest in the play. It looks really funny on stage — the audience can see the characters hiding behind the hedge and can hear them discussing what Malvolio's doing.

Scene Five — Time to Play the Trick on Malvolio

You've had a taster in scenes 2 and 3, but here's where Malvolio shows exactly how pompous and arrogant he is — until the trick makes him look ridiculous.

1 **Toby, Andrew and Fabian are ready for the fun**
Fabian's another servant with an old score to settle against Malvolio. lines 1-12

2 **They hide in the hedge**
Malvolio's coming. Maria tells them to hide in the hedge and drops the letter in the path. lines 13-20

3 **Malvolio already thinks Olivia fancies him**
He thinks she finds him good-looking. lines 21-6

4 **This gets the others quite worked up**
They call him a rogue. Sir Andrew wants to beat him up. lines 27-35

5 **Malvolio fantasises about marrying Olivia**
He'd boss more people around. He'd tell Sir Toby off for drinking and stop him seeing Sir Andrew. lines 36-76

Malvolio's got him into trouble with Olivia in the past.

Why are we hiding behind a giant hedgehog, Sir Toby?
They couldn't find a hedge.
Ask a stupid question.

Sir Toby and Fabian keep shushing each other in case Malvolio hears them.

By this point, Sir Toby's ready to throttle him — Fabian has to hold him back.

Maria wrote some of the letters of Malvolio's name in the poem, so the clues are pretty hard to miss.

Oh, I love it when you smile at me that way. And oh, you look so handsome in those stockings.

6 **Now he sees the letter**
He recognises Olivia's handwriting and the seal on the letter. He decides to read it. lines 77-89

7 **The trick's working**
There's a love poem in the letter, and Malvolio picks up clues that it's about him. The others watch him from the hedge and make comments. lines 90-142

8 **The letter tells Malvolio to do stupid things**
He should be even more pompous. He should be rude to Sir Toby and the servants to prove he loves Olivia. He should wear yellow stockings. lines 143-55

9 **Malvolio falls for it hook, line and sinker**
He's very excited by the letter. He imagines that Olivia really will like his yellow stockings. The letter asks him to smile all the time. lines 156-74

10 **Toby and Fabian think it's hilarious**
Fabian says he wouldn't give this up for a thousand pounds. Toby says he could marry Maria for this. Maria tells them to watch how Malvolio acts in front of Olivia — she's going to hate it. lines 175-202

Malvolio is a gull — I thought that was Albert Ross...

Watch out — this is one of those scenes where you need to know exactly what happens when. It's really important to remember that Malvolio thinks Olivia fancies him before he reads the letter.

Act 3
Scenes 1-2

What Happens in Act Three

Oh dear — this act's all a bit lovey-dovey to start with, but you've still got to know it all.

Scene One — Olivia admits She Loves Viola/Cesario

1 **Viola/Cesario's joking with Feste**
Feste makes a lot of clever jokes and comments. Viola/Cesario joins in. Feste leaves. Viola/Cesario is impressed with his wit. lines 1-64

2 **Sir Toby and Sir Andrew appear**
They're trying to put Viola/Cesario off. Andrew's worried that Olivia likes Cesario. lines 65-87

3 **Olivia wants to see Viola/Cesario alone**
She sends Maria and the others away. Viola/Cesario wants to talk about Orsino's love for Olivia, but Olivia has other ideas. lines 87-106

4 **Olivia tells Viola/Cesario she fancies him**
Viola/Cesario isn't interested, but Olivia keeps on flirting. lines 107-34

5 **Olivia asks what Cesario thinks of her**
Viola/Cesario says Olivia doesn't know what she's doing, then admits that she's pretending to be something she isn't. lines 135-46

6 **Olivia loves Viola/Cesario even more**
She's still smitten, but Viola/Cesario says no woman will be her love. lines 147-66

She understands that Feste must be pretty clever to be able to play the fool so well.

Viola/Cesario tries to put Olivia off, but it only makes things worse:

O, what a deal of scorn looks beautiful
In the contempt and anger of his lip.
(147-8)

= Ooh, he's beautiful when he's angry...

Scene Two — Sir Andrew's Jealous of Cesario

Maria's dead pleased that her plan worked.

1 **Sir Andrew's seen Olivia and Cesario together**
He's upset. Fabian argues that Olivia did it deliberately to make Sir Andrew jealous. lines 1-31

2 **Sir Toby suggests a duel**
He says Olivia will be impressed if Sir Andrew fights Viola/Cesario. Sir Andrew goes off to write a challenge. lines 32-50

3 **Fabian and Sir Toby laugh at Sir Andrew**
Sir Toby tells Fabian he's been living off Andrew's money. They think the idea of Sir Andrew fighting a duel with Cesario is very funny. lines 51-63

4 **Maria's got news about Malvolio**
Malvolio's going about with yellow stockings and a constant grin. Maria says it makes him even more annoying. They all go to watch him. lines 64-81

Andrew's jealous of Cesario — he understands girls so well...

Tricky times for Viola — don't forget this is the first time Olivia's said clearly she loves Cesario.

What Happens in Act Three

Act 3 Scenes 3 & 4

It keeps getting more complicated. Now Sebastian's in town as well as Viola.

Scene Three — Antonio lends Sebastian his Purse

Careful — this scene's dead important for things that happen later in the play.

1. **Antonio's caught up with Sebastian**
   Antonio's followed Sebastian to make sure he's alright. lines 1-19
2. **Sebastian suggests they go sightseeing**
   Antonio refuses — he fought a sea battle against Orsino's ships once. He's afraid he'll be recognised and arrested. lines 20-38
3. **Antonio gives Sebastian his purse**
   He wants Sebastian to buy himself something nice. They arrange to meet at the inn in an hour. Sebastian goes off. lines 38-48

Scene Four — Malvolio Makes a Fool of Himself

Yep — it's the bit you've been waiting for... Malvolio makes a prat of himself.

Malvolio's convinced he's doing the right thing.

Cheer up, mate. She's just playing hard to get.

Making a fool of him is one thing, but locking him up as if he really is mad is pretty cruel.

1. **Olivia's waiting for Cesario**
   She's sad so she sends for Malvolio. Maria says he's acting oddly. lines 1-15
2. **Malvolio comes in smiling**
   Olivia is confused. Malvolio tries to be charming and sexy. lines 16-35
3. **Malvolio brings up the letter**
   He mentions various lines from the letter. Olivia is even more confused. lines 36-55
4. **Olivia doesn't know what he's on about**
   She thinks he's gone mad. She goes to meet Cesario, and leaves Toby to take charge of Malvolio. lines 56-9
5. **Malvolio thinks it's all going his way**
   He's sure it's going to plan. lines 60-77
6. **Sir Toby, Fabian and Maria laugh at him**
   They talk to Malvolio as if he's mad. He's rude to them — like the letter told him to be. lines 78-116
7. **They decide to lock him up**
   They want to keep the joke going for a bit longer. lines 117-30

Love — Malvolio's mad for it...

Watch out — this is a really long act, and it's complicated too. You've still got to know it well though. Turn the page over and scribble down a quick summary of the act so far — then learn it.

Act 3 Scene 4

What Happens in Act Three

This scene's a whopper — it goes on and on. You could get part of this scene in the SAT. You've got to know what happens and when it does, or you could end up in a right muddle.

More Scene Four — Building up to a Fight

Don't fret, just work through the scene bit by bit and you'll get there.

8 Sir Andrew's written his challenge
Sir Toby reads it out and it's dreadful. Sir Toby sends Andrew off the wrong way. Toby won't give Viola/Cesario the letter — it's too badly written to scare anyone. He decides to challenge Cesario by word of mouth instead. lines 131-80

9 Olivia's still trying to charm Viola/Cesario
Olivia gives a picture of herself. Viola/Cesario says it'd be better if she gave her love to Orsino. Olivia leaves. lines 181-99

10 Sir Toby appears, and tries to scare Viola/Cesario
Sir Toby makes Sir Andrew out to be very brave and fierce. lines 200-225

11 Viola/Cesario tries to make excuses
Viola/Cesario really doesn't want to fight, but Toby says there's no way out. Toby leaves but Fabian keeps winding Viola/Cesario up, saying Andrew is a skilled fighter. lines 226-51

What do you think, Sir Toby?
It's truly awful.
It's marvellous.

Viola/Cesario wouldn't have any training in swordfighting because she was a girl — the idea of a duel would be really scary for her.

Come on, man. Stop messing about. I need my purse back.
Sorry, mate. Love to help ya. But I honestly don't know who you are.

Here's where the business about the purse comes in. Antonio thinks that Viola/Cesario is Sebastian, so he asks her for his purse back before he gets carted off to prison.

12 Meanwhile Toby tells Andrew to be afraid
He tells him Cesario is a great fighter. Sir Andrew has second thoughts. lines 252-76

13 They get ready to fight — unwillingly
Viola's almost ready to admit she's a girl. Andrew doesn't want to fight either. lines 277-86

14 Antonio to the rescue!
He mistakes Viola/Cesario for Sebastian. He comes rushing in and threatens Sir Andrew. lines 287-300

15 The police turn up to arrest Antonio
They recognise him from the old battle he fought against Orsino. They arrest him. lines 301-14

16 Antonio asks for his money
He asks for his purse, thinking it's Sebastian, but Viola/Cesario doesn't understand. She offers him some of her own money. Antonio thinks he's been betrayed and curses Sebastian. He is taken away. lines 315-49

17 Hurrah — Viola realises Sebastian must be alive
She realises Antonio thought she was Sebastian, which means her brother might be alive somewhere. lines 350-61

18 Sir Toby thinks Viola/Cesario's a coward
Even Andrew thinks he can beat him now. lines 362-71

A diamond of a fight — a real jewel...

Phew, that was a stonker of a scene to finish off Act Three. Get the order of events in scene 4 good and clear — first the Malvolio stuff, then Toby and the gang, then the challenge and the duel.

What Happens in Act Four

Act 4
Scenes 1, 2 & 3

Phew — you'd think things had got about as muddled as they could get... but you'd be wrong.

Scene One — Sebastian gets Mistaken for Cesario

1. **Feste mistakes Sebastian for Cesario**
   Feste's been sent to get Viola/Cesario. Sebastian doesn't know him and refuses. He gives Feste money. lines 1-23
2. **Sir Andrew attacks Sebastian**
   He hits Sebastian, thinking he's Cesario, but Sebastian hits him back, and draws his dagger. lines 24-6
3. **Sir Toby butts in**
   Toby grabs Sebastian's arm, and Feste goes to get Olivia. Sebastian frees himself, and he and Sir Toby draw their swords. lines 27-43
4. **Olivia arrives just in time**
   She's angry with Toby for fighting Cesario, and sends him away. lines 44-50
5. **She invites Sebastian into the house**
   He's confused, but goes anyway. lines 50-65

What are you doing?
What does it look like?

It's the second time there's nearly been a swordfight in the play — and both times it was interrupted at the last second. A real swordfight's too serious for a comedy.

Scene Two — Another Trick on Malvolio

It's all got a bit nasty now — Malvolio's really suffering.

Well, how can I put this? You're mad. You're a lunatic. You're fruity as a nutcake.

1. **Maria gets Feste to dress up as a priest**
   Feste speaks to Malvolio while Toby watches. He tells Malvolio he's mad even though he says he isn't. lines 1-67
2. **Sir Toby sends Feste as himself**
   Malvolio asks Feste for pen and paper and a candle. He carries on insisting he isn't mad. lines 68-132

Scene Three — Olivia Marries Sebastian in a hurry

1. **Sebastian's having a think**
   He's very confused. Nothing is what it seems to be. He couldn't find Antonio, and now a strange lady has taken a fancy to him. lines 1-21
2. **Olivia comes in with a priest**
   She wants to marry Sebastian. lines 22-31
3. **Sebastian agrees straight away.**
   Off they go into the chapel. lines 32-5

Marriage blues — not until after you're wed...

A lot happens quickly in Act Four — the main thing is Olivia marries Sebastian, thinking he's Cesario.

Act 5 Scene 1

What Happens in Act Five

There's only one scene in this act, but it's a biggie. I've broken it into chunks to make it easier to work through. It's the last bit of the play, where things get sorted out.

Scene One — At Last Orsino Goes to See Olivia

1 Fabian's pestering Feste
Feste's got the letter Malvolio wrote, and Fabian's worried — he wants to see it but Feste won't let him look. lines 1-6

2 Orsino arrives to see Olivia
Orsino's finally decided to see Olivia himself. He turns up with Viola/Cesario. He recognises Feste who jokes with him and gets paid for his efforts. Orsino asks Feste to let Olivia know he's there to see her. lines 7-43

3 Antonio is brought in as a prisoner
Orsino recognises him and says he knows him as a notorious pirate. The officers explain how he was arrested. Viola/Cesario tells the Duke that Antonio saved him earlier, but said some strange things as well. Orsino questions Antonio. lines 44-66

4 Antonio tells his story bitterly
He tells how he rescued Sebastian from the wreck and followed him to Illyria out of love. He thinks he saved Sebastian from Toby and Andrew, but Sebastian refused to give him his own money back. Everyone else is confused when Antonio says he's been with Sebastian for three months — Viola/Cesario has been with the Duke all that time. lines 66-90

The trick on Malvolio's gone a bit too far. Fabian's worried that he'll get into trouble for being part of it.

Need a hand, mate?
That'd be rather nice, thanks.

But Olivia thinks She's Married Cesario

How could you betray me like this?
You've betrayed me. Get lost, I hate you!

5 Olivia appears — things get really complicated
Olivia arrives and ignores Orsino — she wants to know where Cesario's been. Viola/Cesario tries to make her listen to Orsino, but she won't. Orsino moans about her cruelty and decides that Olivia's in love with someone else. He plots revenge on her. He starts to leave and Viola/Cesario follows. lines 91-127

6 Now Olivia gets confused
She asks where Viola/Cesario is going. Viola/Cesario says she's going with Orsino, whom she loves more than anyone else. Olivia sobs she's been betrayed. She asks why her husband is acting this way. lines 128-36

7 Whoops — Orsino goes mental
Orsino is livid. He thinks Viola/Cesario has betrayed him. Olivia has called the priest to remind Cesario of the marriage. Orsino curses Viola/Cesario and says he never wants to see her/him again. Olivia tells Viola/Cesario not to worry. lines 137-65

It's confusing enough for everyone else, but it's horrible for Viola. Everyone's suddenly accusing her of all sorts of things she didn't do.

What Happens in Act Five

Act 5 Scene 1

Just when you thought it couldn't get any worse for Viola/Cesario, in comes Sir Andrew...

Sir Andrew and Sir Toby have been Beaten Up

We don't know what's happened to them yet —
the audience is as much in the dark as all the other characters.

8 Sir Andrew bursts onto the stage
Sir Andrew comes in covered in blood and calling for a surgeon. He tells everyone that he and Toby have been injured by Cesario. Viola/Cesario protests that she's innocent. lines 166-80

9 Sir Toby comes in, helped by Feste
Toby's sober for the first time in the whole play. He's hurt and trying to find a surgeon. Feste tells him the surgeon's drunk and Toby is furious. Sir Andrew offers to help, but Toby turns on him and insults him. They leave the stage. lines 181-97

Well, here's another fine mess you've got us into.

Sebastian Comes Face to Face with Viola/Cesario

This scene's really emotional — neither Viola nor Sebastian can quite believe that the other one is still alive.

10 In comes Sebastian — the penny drops
He apologises to Olivia — it was him who beat up Toby and Andrew. Everyone else looks at him in astonishment. Orsino says he's amazed how alike Sebastian and Cesario are. lines 198-206

11 Sebastian spots Antonio straightaway
He's really happy to see his friend. Antonio asks how Sebastian managed to divide himself in two. Sebastian suddenly sees Viola/Cesario — he's confused too. He says he never had a brother, but did have a sister. He asks Viola/Cesario where she comes from. lines 207-20

It's a ghost!
It's a very strange mirror.

12 Viola's as shocked as Sebastian
She tells Sebastian she's from Messaline, and that her father and brother were called Sebastian, but she's so shocked she asks if Sebastian is a ghost. He tells her he's real, and if she was a woman, he'd know that she was Viola. lines 221-30

13 They realise who the other one is
They swap family details and Viola says she can bring them to the captain who has her female clothes. The whole story is clear to everyone. Sebastian tells Olivia that she nearly married a woman, but luckily she married him. lines 231-52

14 Orsino realises he loves Viola
He tells Olivia not to worry about her mistake, and says that he will have a share in the happiness. He asks Viola about all the times she said she loved him. She promises to swear them over again. Orsino asks to see Viola in her own clothes, but the Captain who had them is in prison because of a legal quarrel with Malvolio. lines 253-66

Hmm — it's convenient that Orsino suddenly falls for Viola, but you've just got to swallow your disbelief, I'm afraid.

Viola and Sebastian — spot the difference...

The very end of the play builds up loads of tension. Everybody's blaming Viola/Cesario for things she didn't do. It's tense because you think she's going to get into real trouble — until Sebastian arrives.

Act 5 Scene 1 (cont.)

What Happens in Act Five

Wow — this scene's neverending. Unfortunately, there's a bit more of the story that needs to be sorted out — Malvolio's still locked up in the loony bin.

Everyone's Forgotten about Malvolio

15 Olivia decides to send for Malvolio
She wants him to release the Captain, but then she remembers that he's been acting madly. She asks Feste how Malvolio is, and Feste offers her Malvolio's letter. She asks him to read it, but Feste keeps making a joke of it, so she tells Fabian to read it instead. lines 267-87

16 The letter doesn't sound mad at all
Malvolio's letter is very clear and calm. He says he's been wronged and that he has the letter that made him act so strangely. Orsino comments that it doesn't sound very mad. Olivia tells Fabian to fetch Malvolio. lines 288-300

17 Olivia offers to hold Orsino's wedding at her house
Orsino agrees, and asks Viola to marry him. Olivia gets excited that Viola will be her sister. lines 301-11

Malvolio Arrives and He's Absolutely Furious

18 Malvolio isn't a happy bunny
He tells Olivia she has wronged him, but she denies it. He shows her the letter and demands to know why he's been treated so badly. Olivia tells him it isn't her writing, it's Maria's. She realises there's been a trick and offers to let Malvolio judge the case. lines 312-40

19 Fabian comes clean about the trick
Fabian tells Olivia that he and Toby set up the trick, and made Maria write the letter. He says that Toby has married Maria for doing it. Fabian tries to say it was a joke rather than anything serious. Olivia sympathises with Malvolio. lines 340-54

20 Feste stirs things up
He reminds Malvolio about some of the things in the letter. He tells Malvolio he was Sir Topas and that he did it as revenge for Malvolio's rudeness about his fooling (see Act 1 Scene 5). lines 355-61

21 Malvolio storms out swearing revenge
He's still furious, and says he'll be revenged on everybody. line 362

22 Orsino sends someone after him
He wants someone to ask Malvolio to make peace. Then he talks about the wedding, and his love for Viola. lines 363-72

23 Feste sings a final song
It's quite sad, about how fooling starts off innocent and ends up lonely. The play's over and he hopes everyone enjoyed it. lines 373- end

This bit's very weird. Everyone else seems to be happy, but Malvolio's threatening revenge.

It feels like the play isn't properly finished.

Revenge and sad songs — a laugh a minute...

This last scene really isn't funny. The Malvolio story ends up nastily, and Feste's song is very sad.

Revision Summary

Blimey — I never knew Twelfth Night was so long. That's why it's important to get this section sorted. In your SAT you'll only get one scene — but you'll do much better if you know where it comes in the story. Think about it — you don't want to be writing about things that happen later in the play as if they've already happened. The examiners will think you don't know what you're talking about. Try these revision questions — see if you can work through all of them without looking back over the section.

1) What do we find out about Orsino in Act 1 Scene 1?
2) What do we find out about Olivia in Act 1 Scene 1?
3) Who washes up in shore on Act 1 Scene 2?
4) What does Maria say about Sir Andrew in Act 1 Scene 2?
5) In which scene do we see Viola dressed as a boy for the first time?
6) Why is Feste in trouble at the start of Act 1 Scene 5?
7) In which act and scene does Viola meet Olivia?
8) In which act and scene do we find out that Viola's brother survived the shipwreck?
9) Why is Viola in a pickle in Act 2 Scene 2?
10) Who breaks up the party in Act 2 Scene 3?
11) What's Maria's cunning plan?
12) Why is the conversation between Orsino and Viola/Cesario in Act 2 Scene 4 funny?
13) Which characters are watching Malvolio read the letter in Act 2 Scene 5?
14) How does Malvolio react when he reads the letter?
15) In which act and scene does Olivia admit she's in love with Viola/Cesario?
16) How does Sir Andrew react when he sees them together?
17) What does Antonio lend to Sebastian in Act 3 Scene 3?
18) In which act and scene does Malvolio make a complete idiot of himself?
19) What happens to him next?
20) Who sets up the fight between Cesario and Sir Andrew?
21) Who comes and stops the fight?
22) Why is Viola so confused when Antonio asks for money?
23) Who does Sir Andrew end up fighting in Act 4 Scene 1?
24) What happens to Sebastian in Act 4 Scene 3?
25) In which act and scene does Orsino finally go to see Olivia?
26) When does everyone work out what's been going on?

So, this chick gets washed up on shore and then she falls in love with the Dukes of Hazzard. Meanwhile some other guys are hiding behind a hedgehog, and there's this mad clown with a festering banjo... no, hang on a minute, that can't be right...
You know, it doesn't smell too good.

Picking Your Task

It all looks a bit confusing at first. The main thing to remember is that you have to read both tasks before you can decide which one you're going to answer.

You Get Two Tasks to Choose From

The first thing you've got to do is read through both of the tasks on your play. Then you need to make up your mind. Don't just pick one because it looks like less work — think about how well you can answer it, too.

Pick a good 'un...

You've only got to do one task — you need to do it as well as you can.

Pick the One You Can Do Best

You'll only have two tasks to choose from. Try and choose the one you'll be able to answer best.

There are lots of different types of task — but you don't know what choice you'll actually get in the SAT. You've got to be ready to answer any type of question.

Ewe gotta choose the best one, & fast!

You could get two tasks like this to choose from:

Act 1 Scenes 1, 2 and 3

TASK 5

Love is one of the main themes of *Twelfth Night*.

How does Shakespeare introduce different kinds of love to the audience in these opening scenes?

If you know the scene or scenes well, you'll be able to write a better answer.

Act 2 Scene 3

TASK 6

In this scene Sir Toby clashes with Malvolio.

What do you learn about the characters of Sir Toby and Malvolio in this scene?

Steer clear of tasks where you don't really understand the question. You could lose a lot of marks if you don't answer the question exactly.

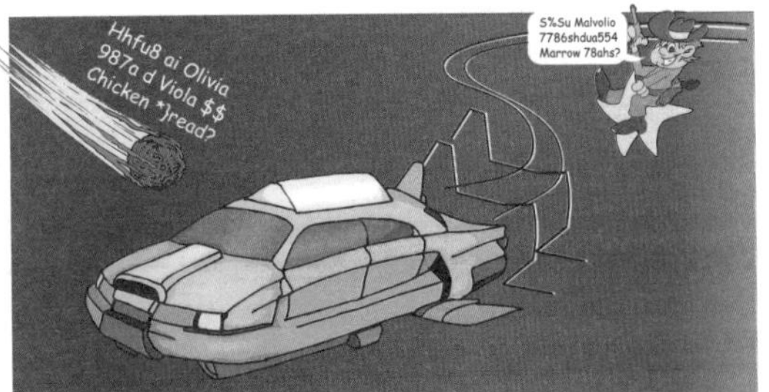

Steer clear of tasks where you don't really understand the question.

Have a really good think about the questions before you make a final decision. You won't have time to change your mind so you need to make the right choice.

Don't choose a question just because you've done one like it in class. If you choose a question that's similar to one you've done before, check for any sneaky little differences.

Beware of different questions in similar disguises

Win a nose-picking contest — pick the best...

The secret of doing well in Paper 2 is reading both tasks carefully before you choose which one you're going to do. Don't just pick the one that looks easier — choose one that you can do well.

Reading the Bit From the Play

This is the really tricky part — reading all that funny lingo. Yep — there's no way round it.

Use These Clues to Help You Read it

1) Check you've got the right play and the right scene — you really don't want to get that wrong.

2) This bit is instructions for people acting in the play — nobody actually says them.

3) This tells you who's speaking.

TWELFTH NIGHT

Act 1 Scene 4

Enter VALENTINE, *and* VIOLA *in man's attire.*

VALENTINE If the Duke continue these favours towards you, Cesario, you are like to be much advanced: he hath known you but three days, and already you are no stranger.

VIOLA You either fear his humour, or my negligence, that you call in question the continuance of his love. Is he inconstant, sir, in his favours?

VALENTINE No, believe me.

4) Here's what each person is saying.

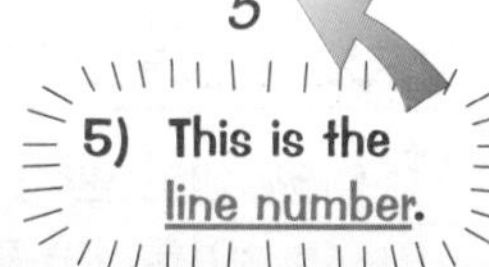

5) This is the line number.

You Must Read through the Whole Thing

It's boring, I'm afraid, but you've got to do it. You'll get about six pages to read. Don't try to skim it — you'll miss loads of important things if you do.

First, go through the passage quickly — just looking at the names of the characters and the stage directions (the bits that tell you what the characters are doing). Jot down some notes on who's in the scene and what happens — that's a good start.

Next, read through the whole thing carefully. Try to work out what it all means (Section Three is all about understanding the weird bits in the language). If you don't understand some of the scene, don't worry — come back to it later.

You'll get 15 minutes to read it and make notes — that's loads of time if you don't waste it.

I dig this play — I read the hole thing...

Don't try to cut corners. The only way you're going to write a decent answer is by reading right through the bit of the play and finding all the things you need to write about. Harsh, but true...

Planning Your Answer

Hmmm — this all seems like a lot of work to me. It doesn't have to be — it's all about knowing what you've got to do before you start writing. That's the only way to get good marks.

Check Exactly What the Task is Asking For

Each task has a list of handy tips to help you with your answer.

How does Shakespeare introduce different kinds of love to the audience in these opening scenes?

Before you begin to write you should think about:

- what Orsino thinks and says about love;
- how different kinds of love are introduced in the scene with Viola and the Captain;
- Sir Toby's attitudes to love and how he speaks about it;
- what the audience learns about Olivia's attitudes to love.

Don't miss anything out — that's just throwing marks away.

The examiners want you to write about all four of these points.

We're done for!
Oh no! Not the handy tips!

You must write about these things in your answer.

Use the Handy Tips to Plan Your Essay

The easiest way to make sure your answer covers all the handy tips is to make notes on all of them as you read the scene. You can use the notes as your plan.

As you read the bit from the play scribble notes on each of the points from the task.

They can be as short and messy as you like — it's only you who has to read them.

You don't want to run out of things to say later — so don't rush into writing. Take time making your notes.

Stick to the order of the handy tips so you don't have to make a separate plan.

1. Orsino
Says in love with Olivia — talks about his feelings, not much about her. A bit fake? (Act 1, Scene 1)
2. Viola & Captain
V loves brother — worried about him.
Also V and Captain friends. (Act 1 Scene 2)
3. Sir T
Teases about Olivia loving Sir A — doesn't take love seriously (Act 1, Scene 3)
4. Olivia
O's brother recently died. Not interested in romantic love at the moment. (Act 1, Scenes 1, 2, & 3)

Make sure you write about all of your points in the 60 minutes. Keep looking at the clock to check there's enough time left.

The SAT is 1 hour and 15 minutes long. Split it up like this:
15 minutes reading and taking notes;
60 minutes writing the answer.

Fingerless gloves — no handy tips there...

It really is ultra-important to make sure you know what you're supposed to write about before you start. If you don't do what the task says, you won't get the marks. That's the simple truth.

Writing Your Answer

Once you've got a plan, you're ready to start writing. Write your answer carefully, though. Remember — you get marked on how well you write.

Write a Simple Opening Paragraph

Use the words of the task.

Do you think I'm too cute to be in this book? I do.

Start by using the exact words of the task in your introduction.

Your introduction doesn't have to be long at all. It's just there to show what your basic answer to the task is.

How does Shakespeare introduce different kinds of love to the audience in these opening scenes?

In the opening scenes of 'Twelfth Night' Shakespeare introduces several different kinds of love. He does it by making the characters speak about their feelings and the feelings of others.

Orsino opens the play talking about love...

Start by leaving a little gap — and do the same for each paragraph.

The first sentence uses the exact words of the task.

The second sentence is a straight answer to the task.

When you've written your opening paragraph, just follow the order of the plan.

Use Lots of Tasty Quotations

Whatever task you choose, you are guaranteed to get better marks if your answer's got some good quotes. Trouble is, you've got to know how to quote properly. Here's how...

Copy down the exact words.

...and the feelings of others.

Orsino opens the play talking about love. He is in love but it sounds like he doesn't want to be:

If music be the food of love, play on,
Give me excess of it, that, surfeiting,
The appetite may sicken and so die.
Act 1, Scene 1, 1-3

Quotes show where your answer comes from.

Start a new paragraph.

Say where the quote comes from. Give the line numbers. If there's more than one scene, give the scene number, too.

Don't quote more than two or three lines at a time.

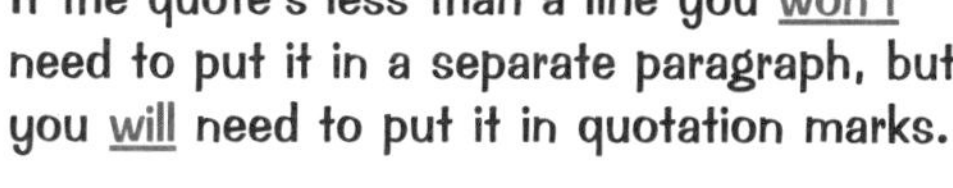

...Love seems to be quite painful for Orsino. He says his feelings for Olivia chase him "like fell and cruel hounds"...

If the quote's less than a line you won't need to put it in a separate paragraph, but you will need to put it in quotation marks.

"Salt and Vinegar" — there's a tasty quote...

The examiners really are dead keen on quoting. If you don't quote at all, you'll get a low mark, no matter how good the rest of your answer is. Don't quote huge chunks, though — you only need a couple of lines to show where your answer comes from. It's all about striking a balance.

Writing Your Answer

This is all about making sure you don't write a load of garbage — it's as simple as that.

Stick to the Point — Don't Just Tell the Story

You don't get marks for writing any old rubbish.
You've got to make sure you're answering the question.

You're just telling the story. You haven't answered the question. Bzzzz BzZZzzz...

Sir Andrew is going to fight Cesario. But Cesario doesn't want to fight. Then Antonio jumps in and saves Cesario...

Lots of people fall into a terrible trap.
They end up re-telling the story of the scenes, without actually answering the question.
If you do that you won't get the marks.

To make sure you're doing the task, keep the words of the question in your mind all the time.

Don't Contradict Yourself — It makes you look Stupid

Another terrible trap is saying one thing, then saying something which means completely the opposite. It makes people sound like they don't know what they're talking about.

> *Sir Toby thinks Sir Andrew is a fool, and only pretends to be his friend, because he has "three thousand ducats a year" (Act 1, Scene 3, 20)...*
> *...Sir Toby is really affectionate to Sir Andrew and calls him "Sweet Sir Andrew!" (line 45)...*

Watch out — these two things can't both be true.

Don't contradict yourself — you'll lose important marks.

Finish Off Your Answer and Check it

You can make your work even better by making sure you finish it off well.

I can't finish it off.
I'll be sick.
Me too.
Ribbit.

1) A definite ending gives you a chance to sum up all your points. It'll impress the examiner, too. It makes your piece look complete.

> *The opening scenes of the play introduce romantic love, love between friends, and love between members of the same family. Some people love in a very genuine way — like the way Viola loves her brother. Others make a show or a joke out of love — like Orsino and Sir Toby.*

Your final paragraph can be really short, just like the opening paragraph.

2) Check to see that the whole answer is written in proper sentences and paragraphs. Check to see that all the spellings are right, especially the names of characters.

3) Don't panic if you run out of time. If there's a point that you haven't covered just bung down a quick sentence about it.

Say no to a gnome — contradict your elf...

Steer clear of the two terrible traps (they're both on this page). When you've finished, check through for daft mistakes. Check those spellings — you really don't want to spell a character's name wrong. An ending paragraph is nice, but if you're pushed for time a sentence will do.

Revision Summary

A whole section of seriously useful tips for your SAT. You'd be madder than a custard cream not to learn that little lot. Use this lovingly crafted Revision Summary to get it all remembered. If you're not sure of an answer, you can go back and check, but don't even think about going on to the next thing until you're getting 'em all 100% right.

1) Is it worth doing a task just because it looks easy?
2) If you don't understand a question, what should you do? *a) Give yourself brain strain until you do understand it b) Give it a miss.*
3) If a question looks similar to one you've done before, what do you need to watch out for?
4) How many pages do you have to read?
5) How much time do you get to read and make notes?
6) When you read the bit from the play, what should you do first?
7) What should you do next?
8) If the task gives you four points to think about, how many do you have to write about? *a) None of them — they're only hints, after all. b) All of them — those examiners aren't kidding. c) One or two — you don't want to overdo it.*
9) What's the easiest way to make sure your essay covers all the points in the task?
10) Do you have to do a separate plan?
11) Do your notes have to be nice and neat?
12) What should you put in your first paragraph?
13) Should an introduction be: *a) long and rambling?* or *b) short and to the point?*
14) How should you put your main points in order?
15) What guarantees you better marks? *a) Using quotations. b) Sellotaping £20 to your exam paper. c) Copying your answer out of the Oxford Companion to English Literature.*
16) How many lines should you quote at a time?
17) If you quote less than one line, what punctuation marks do you need to use?
18) What are the two terrible traps that people fall into?
19) What three things should you do when you finish your answer off?
20) What should you do if you run out of time?

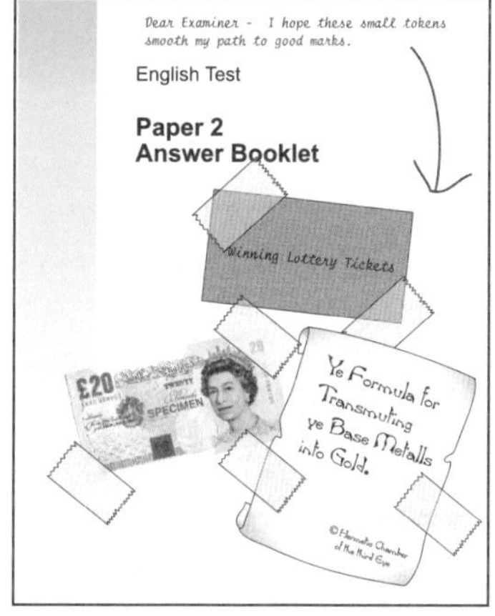

One of these will help you get more marks in the test...

Writing About Characters

This is the easiest kind of task you can get in the SAT. You have to write about one of the characters in the scene. It's pretty straightforward — as long as you follow the method.

Writing About Characters Isn't that Tricky

Here's a typical task asking you to write about a character.

Act 1 Scene 5, line 160 to the end of the scene, and Act 2 Scene 2

What problems does Viola face, and how does she react to them in these scenes?

Watch out — there are two bits to this task.

Before you begin to write you should think about:

- the reason why Viola has been sent to see Olivia;
- Viola's conversation with Olivia;
- what Olivia says to herself about Cesario;
- Viola's situation at the end of these scenes.

These bits are brilliant — they tell you what to write about. Make sure you do all four of them.

You Need to Do Two Things

This question's asking what problems Viola has and how she reacts.

Hello Thing
Hello Thing
TWO THINGS

1. You've got to say what her problems are at the start and the end of the scenes — and what happens in between to change them.
2. You also have to say how Viola reacts to these problems — what she says and what she does.

Her Reaction is about How as well as What

What

1) You should look at what she says — and how she says it.

Viola says to Olivia, "I am not that I play" (line 176) — she isn't what she seems to be. She doesn't say it directly though, but as a throwaway comment. The audience understands that it's a joke, but Olivia doesn't.

How

2) But don't forget to think about what she doesn't say as well.

Viola doesn't tell Olivia that she's a woman in disguise. If she did, Olivia wouldn't make the mistake of falling in love with Viola.

3) Look at what she does too.

She refuses to take money from Olivia, saying she's not a "fee'd post," a mere servant.

Long John Silver — writing a-boat character...

These tasks aren't too difficult — as long as you work out all the parts you've got to do.

Writing About Characters

The secret of these questions is making sure you work through all of the points from the task. You don't want to leave any out — you'd be throwing away lots of lovely marks.

You've Got to Look at Olivia as well as Viola

Be careful — the task is asking about Viola, but one bit of it is about Olivia.

Olive...Olivia. Fantastic joke... I don't how you do it..... not.

- what Olivia says to herself about Cesario;

Make sure you link it to the main bit of the task.

Viola's biggest problem in this scene is that Olivia falls in love with her. All Viola has tried to do is be honest and do what Orsino asked. Unfortunately, Olivia mistakes what she says. When Olivia is alone she remembers exactly what Viola said to her;

Give plenty of quotes to back up your points.

"Above my fortunes, yet my state is well;
I am a gentleman." I'll be sworn thou art; (lines 277-8)

Olivia is convinced that Viola is more noble than she's letting on. When Viola refuses the money Olivia offers, she tells Olivia to "keep your purse." All of this makes Olivia think that Cesario comes from the same social class as her. That would mean there would be no problem for them to get married.

Don't Forget to Talk about Viola's Reaction

That means looking at her reaction to Olivia, her reaction to Malvolio when he brings the ring, and what she says to the audience when she's on her own (what she really thinks).

1) This is about Viola's reaction to Olivia.

Viola delivers the message from Orsino as best she can. She goes out of her way to be polite, especially at the end of their conversation. Olivia offers her money, but Viola refuses, saying that it's Orsino, not her, who wants a reward: "My master, not myself, lacks recompense." (line 272) Viola's reaction gives Olivia the wrong idea, however.

I got you a ring, but I wasn't sure of your size.

Not quite the reaction I was expecting.
POW!

2) And here's her reaction to Malvolio.

When Malvolio is sent to give Viola the ring, her reaction is one of confusion. Malvolio is downright rude, "You might have saved me my pains, to have taken it away yourself." (Act 2, scene 2, lines 4-5). Viola is indignant: "She took the ring of me, I'll none of it." (line 11)

3) Then there's what she really thinks.

Left alone, Viola turns to the audience in confusion: "I left no ring with her. What means this lady?" (line 16) Then she starts to work it out, "Fortune forbid my outside have not charmed her!". She realises that Olivia has fallen in love with her.

A task about Viola — that's a real test of character...

Get this clear — don't leave out any reactions from the scene. And don't forget the other characters.

Writing as a Director

Here's something a bit more difficult — writing as the director of the play. You've got to imagine you're telling people how to act the scene out on stage, and bring it to life for anyone watching.

You Get Marked on Reading and Writing Just the Same

Careful — these tasks look completely different from the others, but they're marked on exactly the same things. They're about how well you read the scene and how well you write about it.

Act 2 Scene 5

Imagine you are going to direct this scene for a class performance.

Explain how you want the pupil playing Malvolio to show his responses to the letter and how you want the pupils playing Sir Toby, Sir Andrew and Fabian to react to the trick.

Before you begin to write you should decide what advice to give the actors about:

- how you want Malvolio to speak and to behave before he finds the letter;
- how you want Malvolio to behave when he reads the letter;
- how to use Malvolio's language to show his thoughts and feelings in this scene;
- how you want Sir Toby, Sir Andrew and Fabian to react to the things Malvolio says.

It's asking you for your opinion.

DIRECTOR

Now respond to the letter!

Here's what you need to do.

WARNING: these tasks are seriously tricky — you need to know the scene really well to get decent marks.

You Need to Tell the Actors Two Things

1. You've got to tell the actors how to say their lines — so you need to know what everything means.

Don't forget to quote the lines — or you won't get the marks.

In the first part of the scene, Malvolio is imagining what it would be like to be married to Olivia. He imagines what he would say to Sir Toby: "Cousin Toby, my fortunes, having cast me on your niece, give me this prerogative of speech—".

The language is formal and elegant, but the actor should make it sound arrogant and proud coming from Malvolio. He's got ideas above his station so he should make the speech to Sir Toby completely over the top.

2. You also have to tell them what to do on the stage — how they should move around, and where they should stand.

When Malvolio says, "You must amend your drunkenness", the actor should wag his finger and act as if he really is talking to Sir Toby. This would be even funnier if he does it in the direction of the place where the audience knows Toby is actually hiding.

The actor playing Sir Toby should appear furious at this and say, "Out, scab!" quite loudly. The actor playing Fabian should have to hold him back to stop him rushing to attack Malvolio and spoiling the whole trick.

Use the stage directions to help you too.

Mood Tasks

Mood tasks ask how a scene makes you feel. They usually ask you to explain how Shakespeare gives a scene a particular atmosphere.

Mood Tasks Look Nasty — But They Aren't that Bad

The key thing about these tasks is they're not just about the characters or the story — they're about how the members of the audience feel when they watch the scene, and why they feel like that.

Act 2 Scene 5

Explain how Shakespeare makes this scene funny.

Before you begin to write you should think about:

- what Malvolio, Sir Toby and Sir Andrew are like;
- how Malvolio falls for the trick played on him;
- the language Malvolio uses in this scene;
- how Sir Toby and the others react to what Malvolio says.

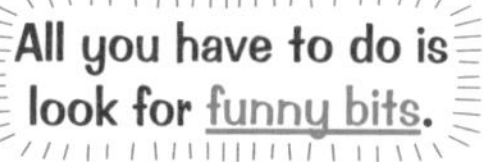
All you have to do is
look for funny bits.

English
Key Stage Three
SAT

Yeah, he looks nasty,
but he's really not that bad

Focus on How the Audience Feels

1) This bit's about what Malvolio is like — how Shakespeare shows the audience his character.

The audience
feels great!

The main reason this scene is funny is because Shakespeare shows us just how ridiculous Malvolio is. When he imagines himself telling Toby to "amend your drunkenness" (line 69), he looks and sounds unbelievably pompous. This means that when he finds the letter and is tricked by it, the audience finds it really funny — they feel he deserves to be made a fool of.

2) You need to explain how Malvolio falls for the trick — it's one of the funniest things in the scene.

The trick is also funny because Malvolio falls for it completely. At the beginning of the scene he imagines that Olivia really does have feelings for him. He says that Maria told him so: "Maria once told me she did affect me, and I have heard herself come thus near, that should she fancy, it should be one of my complexion" (lines 22-24). He believes Olivia loves him even before reading the letter.

3) All the way through you've got to say why the audience finds the scene funny.

Shakespeare manages to make the audience feel like they're part of the trick. The joke is on Malvolio because we all know something he doesn't. That means the audience is laughing at him for believing it. The only reason we don't mind laughing at Malvolio is because he comes across as a really unpleasant and proud character — the audience wants to see him get his come-uppance.

This spleen is
hilarious.

Paxman talks bull — he asks lots of moo-ed questions...

Hurrah — a type of task that's easier than it looks. It's all to do with how the audience feels.

Mood Tasks

Uh oh, here's the tricky bit — looking at the things that make the audience feel the mood.

You've Got to Write About the Language

Have a think about whether the scene's in poetry or prose — and why.

Talk about what the language is like.

Embraced by blood and spirit? Eeeurgh!

Twelfth Night Tonight

This scene is in prose, which shows straightaway that it's meant to be comic. At the same time, the language Malvolio uses, and the language of the letter, are very formal sounding and exaggerated. The letter sounds really poetic, as if Olivia had written it, but it isn't in poetry. It isn't what it seems to be: "Thy Fates open their hands; let thy blood and spirit embrace them," (lines 139-40).

Sir Toby, Sir Andrew and Fabian speak in much less overblown language...

Give plenty of examples too.

Think About How the Scene Could be Acted

This is where you can really pick up marks.
Most people forget to write about acting the scene on stage.

Look for clues in the language — sometimes characters say things that tell you what they're doing.

As Malvolio imagines himself married to Olivia, the scene could be made funnier by Malvolio acting out his fantasy. Shakespeare hints at this in the text of the scene, where he has Malvolio saying, "I extend my hand to him thus, quenching my familiar smile with an austere regard of control —" (line 62-3). Malvolio would stretch out his hand as he said this, in a very slow and over-the-top way, and his face would change from a smile to a proud and cross look.

In other words, Shakespeare tells the actor how to move and pull a funny face to make the audience laugh...

Act with your face, not with a plaice!

And How the Other Characters React to Malvolio

Malvolio's wandering around the stage — but think about what the other characters say and do while the scene's going on.

You need to put yourself in the position of the audience.

One reason the scene is funny to watch is that the audience can see Sir Toby, Sir Andrew and Fabian hiding on the stage. They aren't just watching Malvolio — they're watching the reactions of the other characters. Neither Sir Toby nor Sir Andrew can resist commenting on whatever Malvolio says. Fabian has to keep shutting them up: "O, peace, peace, peace! Now, now." (line 54).

When Malvolio imagines himself talking to Sir Toby, he talks about the people who Toby spends time with: "Besides, you waste the treasure of your time with a foolish knight —" (lines 72-3). Sir Andrew can't resist saying, "That's me, I warrant you." Malvolio continues, "One Sir Andrew —"; Andrew comments happily, "I knew 'twas I, for many do call me fool." (line 76). It's as if they're having a conversation — and it's funny because Andrew recognises that everyone thinks he's a fool, but doesn't realise he actually is one.

Re-action — that's when they say "take two"...

Don't forget to write about the language and how the scene could be acted to make it funny.

Tasks on How the Scene is Written

These are pretty similar to mood tasks — they're all about how Shakespeare tells the audience something in a scene or a group of scenes.

You Have to Do Loads for Tasks like This One

Uh oh — this one looks simpler than you think.

Watch it — you've got three short scenes with lots of different characters to look at, not one long one with two or three characters.

Act 1 Scenes 1, 2, 3

This is a very rare kind of love, commonly known as "chess-piece-love".

How does Shakespeare introduce different kinds of love to the audience in these opening scenes?

You're not just looking for one thing either. You've got to look for more than one kind of love.

Before you begin to write you should think about:

- what Orsino thinks and says about love;
- how different kinds of love are introduced in the scene with Viola;
- Sir Toby's attitudes to love and how he speaks it;
- what the audience learns about Olivia's attitudes to love.

It's about How Shakespeare Makes You Notice Things

1) Start by finding as many different kinds of love as you can. Then you'll need examples for each one — which means quoting.

Scene 1: *Orsino's love for Olivia — The description of Olivia's love for her dead brother.*
Scene 2: *Viola's love for Sebastian (family love) — the love of friends like the Captain... etc.*

2) But that's not all you've got to do. You have to write about how Shakespeare introduces these kinds of love — how he makes the audience notice them.

Shakespeare introduces the idea of family love when Valentine reports back to Orsino. He tells the Duke that Olivia is mourning for her dead brother, and will not stop for seven years:

all this to season
A brother's dead love, which she would keep fresh
And lasting, in her sad remembrance. *(Scene 1, 30-32)*

Olivia's wish to keep her brother's love fresh sounds really beautiful. She doesn't want to go out into the world because she misses him so much. At the same time, it's very unhealthy. Olivia seems to be enjoying being miserable, just like Orsino is enjoying being miserable in love.

3) This bit's about the first thing the audience learns about Olivia.

Don't forget to cover all the points in the task.

Keep your love fresh — brush your teeth before kissing...

Blimey — watch out for these tasks. They're extra difficult because they don't just ask for one thing.

Writing as a Character

OK, this is the kind of task you need to be really wary about. Writing as if you're one of the characters in the scene looks like a dead easy option. But here's the bad news — it isn't.

It's About the Character's Thoughts and Feelings

You have to do all the same things as for any other task — and you've got to stay in character as well.

Act 3 Scene 4, line 200 to end & Act 4 Scene 1

Imagine you are Sir Toby. Describe your thoughts and feelings at the end of these two scenes.

You could begin: *A plague on this Cesario! One minute he's as timid as a mouse, the next he's fighting like a lion...*

Before you start writing you should think about:

- how the fight between Cesario and Sir Andrew was arranged;
- the result of Antonio's interruption;
- the change in Cesario between the two fights;
- Olivia's reaction to the fight with Cesario.

You've Got to Write As If You're Sir Toby

There's a real knack to these tasks — they're not as much fun as they look.

1. You need to think about what the character is like and how he would speak — you have to sound just like him.

This is the sort of thing Toby would say.

This Cesario is a scurvy knave. If I ever meet him on a dark night, I'll teach him a lesson he'll never forget!

2. You've also got to think about where these scenes come in the story. Sir Toby still thinks that Viola and Sebastian are the same person, Cesario.

He wouldn't understand why Cesario seems so different from one minute to the next.

Become the character
Think as they think,
feel how they feel.

When I first spoke with Cesario, he seemed terrified, "I am no fighter." He fell for the trick straightaway and showed his inexperience. "I do assure you, 'tis against my will." That was what he said — the words of a coward! He even seemed scared of Andrew! How could anyone be scared of that fool?

Then five minutes later, we met him again and suddenly he turned vicious. He walloped Andrew good and proper, "Why, there's for thee, and there, and there." He broke out of my hold and drew his sword on me! On me! The same boy who was frightened of Andrew before! It's like he was a different person...

Even though Sir Toby doesn't know the truth, he could easily say something like this as a throwaway comment — you'd get valuable marks for being clever here.

An actor's dilemma — Toby or not Toby...

Remember — think about what the character's like and how well they understand what's going on.

Revision Summary

OK — that's what you're up against in the SATs. Any two of the types of task in this Section could come up in your exam. The secret is to be prepared for any of them. Don't go into the exam expecting one kind of task to turn up — maybe it won't. As long as you're ready for anything, you'll have a great chance of doing well. Have a go at these revision questions now — they're all about seeing what you know and what you need to work on. The more work you do now, the easier things'll be when it gets to the real thing.

1) Which are the easiest kind of tasks you can get in the SAT?
2) What do you have to write about if the task asks "how someone reacts"?
3) What do you get marked on for directing tasks?
4) What two things do you have to tell the actors?
5) Can you use the stage directions to help you?
6) What do mood tasks ask you about?
7) Name two things you can write about that make the audience feel the mood.
8) Why are tasks on how the scene is written difficult?
9) Do you need to cover all the points in the task?
10) Do you have to do the same things as for any other task when you're writing as a character?
11) What two things do you need to think about if you want to sound like a character?
12) Why do you need to know where the scene comes in the story?
13) Does the character understand everything that's going on?

Reading the Key Scenes

Here comes the final section — with all the most important scenes from the play. These are the ones most likely to come up in the SAT so read and enjoy — well, read them anyway.

You Need to Understand as Much as Possible

1) You've got to get to know these scenes better than your own name. That way the weasly examiners won't be able to spring any nasty surprises on you in the SAT.

KS 3
Shakespeare
SATS
It's horrible in there — don't go in!
Doesn't bother me, love. I've seen it all before.

2) You don't want to spend half your reading time in the SAT wondering what on earth the characters are babbling on about. Use this section to get a grip on what the words really mean.

3) Nobody understands every single word Shakespeare wrote — not even the crustiest old actors. It's OK if you don't understand everything in the play. Just aim to understand as much as possible.

These Little Bits are Here to Help You

The text's got lots of lovely helpful bits stuck on to make it easier to read.

ACT 2 SCENE 5
Olivia's garden

Enter SIR TOBY, SIR ANDREW *and* FABIAN

SIR TOBY Come thy ways, Signior Fabian.

FABIAN Nay, I'll come. If I lose a scruple of this sport, let me be boiled to death with melancholy.

SIR TOBY Wouldst thou not be glad to have the niggardly rascally sheep-biter come by some notable shame?

FABIAN I would exult, man. You know he brought me out o' favour with my lady about a bear-baiting here.

SIR TOBY To anger him, we'll have the bear again; and we will fool him black and blue, shall we not, Sir Andrew?

SIR ANDREW And we do not, it is pity of our lives.

SIR TOBY Here comes the little villain.

Enter MARIA

Maria sets up the trick on Malvolio. Sir Toby, Fabian and Sir Andrew watch him fall for it.

1 'Hurry up, Fabian.'

2-3 'I'm coming. I'd rather die of melancholy than miss this.'

scrap

4-5 'Wouldn't it be great to see that rotten Malvolio get seriously shown up?'

10 'If we didn't, we wouldn't deserve to live.'

The clouds give you a quick overview of what happens in each scene.

These boxes explain a tricky word in the text.

This is explaining a whole sentence from the text. The colour of the line numbers matches the colour of the text.

Sir Andrew's been made a rather tasty pink for this scene.

Don't forget to look at all the usual helpful bits. The stage directions tell you when characters come on and off and where the scene's set.

I think it rather suits me.

Don't you think it's a touch passé?

A play about locksmiths — lots of key scenes...

Cor blimey. Time to get really stuck into the play. The better you know the key scenes, the better your chances are in the SAT. Read each scene as many times as you can stand. To liven things up read the scenes aloud with a couple of mates, then test each other on what happened. Go on — it'll definitely improve your grade, believe you me.

Orsino says how much he loves Olivia, but is told she is mourning her brother's death for seven years. Bad luck Orsino.

Twelfth Night
ACT 1 SCENES 1–3
Orsino's palace

[Music] Enter ORSINO, Duke of Illyria, CURIO, and other LORDS

ORSINO If music be the food of love, play on;
Give me excess of it, that, surfeiting,
The appetite may sicken, and so die.
That strain again, it had a dying fall;
O, it came o'er my ear like the sweet sound
That breathes upon a bank of violets,
Stealing and giving odour. Enough; no more.
'Tis not so sweet now as it was before.
O spirit of love, how quick and fresh art thou,
That, notwithstanding thy capacity,
Receiveth as the sea. Nought enters there,
Of what validity and pitch soe'er,
But falls into abatement and low price
Even in a minute. So full of shapes is fancy,
That it alone is high fantastical.

CURIO Will you go hunt, my lord?

ORSINO What, Curio?

CURIO The hart.

ORSINO Why so I do, the noblest that I have.
O, when mine eyes did see Olivia first,
Methought she purged the air of pestilence;
That instant was I turned into a hart,
And my desires like fell and cruel hounds
E'er since pursue me.
[Enter VALENTINE] How now, what news from her?

VALENTINE So please my lord, I might not be admitted,
But from her handmaid do return this answer:
The element itself, till seven years' heat,
Shall not behold her face at ample view;
But like a cloistress she will veilèd walk,
And water once a day her chamber round
With eye-offending brine; all this to season
A brother's dead love, which she would keep fresh
And lasting, in her sad remembrance.

ORSINO O she that hath a heart of that fine frame
To pay this debt of love but to a brother,
How will she love, when the rich golden shaft
Hath killed the flock of all affections else
That live in her; when liver, brain, and heart,
These sovereign thrones, are all supplied and filled
Her sweet perfections with one selfsame king!

2-4 'Give me enough to make my love so sick of it, that it dies. Play that bit again — it was cool.'

7-8 'Stop it — it's not so good anymore.'

10-11 'Love is like the sea, devouring everything. Nothing can satisfy it.'

love

male deer (pun on heart)

plague

19-23 'It was love at first sight. Since then thoughts of her have followed me everywhere.'

24-32 'They wouldn't let me in, but her maid (Maria) told me she won't show her face for seven years. She'll hide away like a nun and cry bitter tears for her brother.'

Cupid's arrow

33-9 'If she can love a brother that much, think what she'll be like when she falls in love with me.'

sexual desire, thoughts & feelings

Away before me to sweet beds of flowers:
Love-thoughts lie rich when canopied with bowers. *Exeunt*

SCENE 2
The coast of Illyria

Enter VIOLA, a CAPTAIN, and SAILORS

VIOLA What country, friends, is this?

CAPTAIN This is Illyria, lady.

VIOLA And what should I do in Illyria?
My brother, he is in Elysium.
Perchance he is not drowned: what think you, sailors?

CAPTAIN It is perchance that you yourself were saved.

VIOLA O my poor brother! And so perchance may he be.

CAPTAIN True, madam, and to comfort you with chance,
Assure yourself, after our ship did split,
When you, and those poor number saved with you,
Hung on our driving boat, I saw your brother
Most provident in peril, bind himself
(Courage and hope both teaching him the practice)
To a strong mast that lived upon the sea;
Where like Arion on the dolphin's back
I saw him hold acquaintance with the waves
So long as I could see.

VIOLA For saying so, there's gold.
Mine own escape unfoldeth to my hope,
Whereto thy speech serves for authority,
The like of him. Know'st thou this country?

CAPTAIN Ay, madam, well, for I was bred and born
Not three hours' travel from this very place.

VIOLA Who governs here?

CAPTAIN A noble duke in nature as in name.

VIOLA What is his name?

CAPTAIN Orsino.

VIOLA Orsino! I have heard my father name him.
He was a bachelor then.

CAPTAIN And so is now, or was so very late;
For but a month ago I went from hence,
And then 'twas fresh in murmur (as you know
What great ones do, the less will prattle of)
That he did seek the love of fair Olivia.

VIOLA What's she?

CAPTAIN A virtuous maid, the daughter of a count
That died some twelvemonth since, then leaving her

Viola's worried about her brother. The captain tells her about Orsino and Olivia. She decides to disguise herself as a man and serve Orsino.

4-5 'My brother's in heaven, unless he didn't drown.'

6 'It was only luck that saved you.'

EEEEEK!

bloke saved from drowning by a dolphin in Greek mythology

19-21 'My own escape and what you have said give me hope that my brother is still alive.'

29 'He was single then.'

31-4 'When I left there was a rumour that Orsino was trying to get in with Olivia.'

40-41 'She has sworn not to look at or mix with men.'

41-44 'I wish I could work for her and hide away until I have decided what to do.'

44-6 'That'll be hard to bring about — she won't listen to anyone's requests, not even Orsino's.'

No suits!

She never lets me in.

In the protection of his son, her brother,
Who shortly also died; for whose dear love
(They say) she hath abjured the sight
And company of men.

VIOLA O that I served that lady,
And might not be delivered to the world
Till I had made mine own occasion mellow
What my estate is!

CAPTAIN That were hard to compass,
Because she will admit no kind of suit,
No, not the duke's.

VIOLA There is a fair behaviour in thee, captain,
And though that nature with a beauteous wall
Doth oft close in pollution, yet of thee
I well believe thou hast a mind that suits
With this thy fair and outward character.
I prithee (and I'll pay thee bounteously)
Conceal me what I am, and be my aid
For such disguise as haply shall become
The form of my intent. I'll serve this duke.
Thou shalt present me as an eunuch to him –
It may be worth thy pains – for I can sing,
And speak to him in many sorts of music
That will allow me very worth his service.
What else may hap, to time I will commit,
Only shape thou thy silence to my wit.

CAPTAIN Be you his eunuch, and your mute I'll be;
When my tongue blabs, then let mine eyes not see.

VIOLA I thank thee. Lead me on. *Exeunt*

47-55 'You appear to be good, but appearances can be deceptive. I trust you anyway. Help me disguise myself as a man.'

60-61 'I'll wait and see what happens, but for now don't tell anyone.'

63 'I'd go blind rather than spill the beans.'

SCENE 3
Olivia's house

Maria complains about Sir Toby's drunkenness and says Sir Andrew is foolish. Sir Andrew proves it, decides to stay and boasts of his dancing skills.

Enter SIR TOBY BELCH and MARIA

SIR TOBY What a plague means my niece to take the death of her brother thus? I am sure care's an enemy to life.

MARIA By my troth, Sir Toby, you must come in earlier o' nights. Your cousin, my lady, takes great exceptions to your ill hours.

SIR TOBY Why, let her except, before excepted.

MARIA Ay, but you must confine yourself within the modest limits of order.

SIR TOBY Confine? I'll confine my self no finer than I am: these clothes are good enough to drink in, and so be these boots too; and they be not, let them hang themselves in their own straps.

1-2 'Olivia's mourning spoils all our fun.'

4-5 'Olivia doesn't like you coming in late at night.'

6 'She can object if she likes.'

7-8 'But you've got to control yourself.'

MARIA That quaffing and drinking will undo you: I heard my lady talk of it yesterday and of a foolish knight that you brought in one night here to be her wooer.

SIR TOBY Who, Sir Andrew Aguecheek?

MARIA Ay, he.

SIR TOBY He's as tall a man as any's in Illyria.

MARIA What's that to th' purpose?

SIR TOBY Why, he has three thousand ducats a year.

MARIA Ay, but he'll have but a year in all these ducats. He's a very fool and a prodigal.

SIR TOBY Fie, that you'll say so! He plays o' th' viol-de-gamboys, and speaks three or four languages word for word without book, and hath all the good gifts of nature.

MARIA He hath indeed all, most natural: for besides that he's a fool, he's a great quarreller; and but that he hath the gift of a coward to allay the gust he hath in quarrelling, 'tis thought among the prudent he would quickly have the gift of a grave.

SIR TOBY By this hand, they are scoundrels and substractors that say so of him. Who are they?

MARIA They that add, moreover, he's drunk nightly in your company.

SIR TOBY With drinking healths to my niece! I'll drink to her as long as there is a passage in my throat and drink in Illyria; he's a coward and a coistrill that will not drink to my niece till his brains turn o' th' toe like a parish top. What, wench! *Castiliano vulgo:* for here comes Sir Andrew Agueface.

Enter SIR ANDREW [AGUECHEEK]

SIR ANDREW Sir Toby Belch! How now, Sir Toby Belch?

SIR TOBY Sweet Sir Andrew!

SIR ANDREW Bless you, fair shrew.

MARIA And you too, sir.

SIR TOBY Accost, Sir Andrew, accost.

SIR ANDREW What's that?

SIR TOBY My niece's chambermaid.

SIR ANDREW Good Mistress Accost, I desire better acquaintance.

MARIA My name is Mary, sir.

SIR ANDREW Good Mistress Mary Accost –

SIR TOBY You mistake, knight. 'Accost' is front her, board her, woo her, assail her.

13 'Your drunkenness will be your downfall.'

brave

21 'All that money will only last him a year.'

musical instrument

24-5 'He's learnt 3 or 4 languages — but by copying, not from books.'

26-30 'He's a simpleton, and an argumentative fool. If he wasn't such a coward, he would've been killed yonks ago.'

33-4 'They also say he gets drunk every night with you.'

35-38 'But only through drinking toasts to Olivia. Anyone who wouldn't drink to her until their head spins like a whipping top is a worthless coward.'

straight faces

ATI... SHOO!

A Fair Shrew

pay her a compliment

personal servant

Sir Toby keeps going on about 'accosting' here. He's making lots of saucy gags about flirting with Maria.

SIR ANDREW By my troth, I would not undertake her in this company. Is that the meaning of 'accost'?

MARIA Fare you well, gentlemen.

SIR TOBY And thou let part so, Sir Andrew, would thou mightst never draw sword again.

SIR ANDREW And you part so, mistress, I would I might never draw sword again. Fair lady, do you think you have fools in hand?

MARIA Sir, I have not you by th' hand.

SIR ANDREW Marry, but you shall have, and here's my hand.

MARIA Now, sir, thought is free. I pray you bring your hand to th' buttery-bar and let it drink.

SIR ANDREW Wherefore, sweetheart? What's your metaphor?

MARIA It's dry, sir.

SIR ANDREW Why, I think so: I am not such an ass but I can keep my hand dry. But what's your jest?

MARIA A dry jest, sir.

SIR ANDREW Are you full of them?

MARIA Ay, sir, I have them at my fingers' ends; marry, now I let go your hand, I am barren. *Exit*

SIR TOBY O knight, thou lack'st a cup of canary. *[Hands him a cup]* When did I see thee so put down?

SIR ANDREW Never in your life, I think, unless you see canary put me down. Methinks sometimes I have no more wit than a Christian or an ordinary man has, but I am a great eater of beef, and I believe that does harm to my wit.

SIR TOBY No question.

SIR ANDREW And I thought that, I'd forswear it. I'll ride home tomorrow, Sir Toby.

SIR TOBY *Pourquoi,* my dear knight?

SIR ANDREW What is *'pourquoi'?* Do, or not do? I would I had bestowed that time in the tongues that I have in fencing, dancing, and bear-baiting. O, had I but followed the arts!

SIR TOBY Then hadst thou had an excellent head of hair.

SIR ANDREW Why, would that have mended my hair?

SIR TOBY Past question, for thou seest it will not curl by nature.

SIR ANDREW But it becomes me well enough, does't not?

SIR TOBY Excellent; it hangs like flax on a distaff; and I hope to see a housewife take thee between her legs and spin it off.

SIR ANDREW Faith, I'll home tomorrow, Sir Toby; your niece will not be seen, or if she be, it's four to one, she'll none of me. The count himself here hard by woos her.

SIR TOBY She'll none o' th' count; she'll not match above her degree, neither in estate, years, nor wit. I have heard her swear't. Tut, there's life in't, man.

SIR ANDREW I'll stay a month longer. I am a fellow o' th' strangest mind i' th' world; I delight in masques and revels sometimes altogether.

SIR TOBY Art thou good at these kickshawses, knight?

SIR ANDREW As any man in Illyria, whatsoever he be, under the degree of my betters, and yet I will not compare with an old man.

SIR TOBY What is thy excellence in a galliard, knight?

SIR ANDREW Faith, I can cut a caper.

SIR TOBY And I can cut the mutton to't.

SIR ANDREW And I think I have the back-trick simply as strong as any man in Illyria.

SIR TOBY Wherefore are these things hid? Wherefore have these gifts a curtain before 'em? Are they like to take dust, like Mistress Mall's picture? Why dost thou not go to church in a galliard and come home in a coranto? My very walk should be a jig; I would not so much as make water but in a sink-a-pace. What dost thou mean? Is it a world to hide virtues in? I did think, by the excellent constitution of thy leg, it was formed under the star of a galliard.

SIR ANDREW Ay, 'tis strong, and it does indifferent well in a dun-coloured stock. Shall we set about some revels?

SIR TOBY What shall we do else? Were we not born under Taurus?

SIR ANDREW Taurus? That's sides and heart.

SIR TOBY No, sir, it is legs and thighs. Let me see thee caper. Ha, higher! Ha, ha, excellent! *Exeunt*

---

goodbye, farewell

←Fools

to deal with

By the Virgin Mary!

Why?

empty

Do you think all this beef is making me stupid?

sweet wine from Canary Islands

78-81 'Sometimes I think I might not be that bright. Maybe it's because I eat too much beef.'

why

86-7 'I wish I'd spent more time learning languages'

94 'It suits me well enough, doesn't it?'

linen on a spindle for making thread

98-100 'By heck, I'll go home tomorrow. Olivia's not seeing anyone and certainly not me. Orsino's trying to woo her too.'

101-3 'She won't marry anyone with a higher title, or older or cleverer than her — so you're still in with a chance, mate.'

fancy dress parties

celebrations

silly things

galliard, coranto, jig, and sink-a-pace are all types of dance

112 'By God, I can jump.'

jump, also a spice eaten with mutton

116-17 'Why do you keep your skill at dancing hidden?'

122-4 'Looking at your leg, I'd say you were born for dancing?'

125-6 'Yep, my leg's strong, and it looks ace in a brown stocking. Let's party.'

129 Each star sign was thought to control a different part of the body.

Feste comes to ask Olivia to take him on as her Fool again. Malvolio tries to put her off. Viola/Cesario comes with a message from Orsino — but Olivia's more interested in the messenger.

ACT 1 SCENE 5
Olivia's house

Enter MARIA and FESTE

MARIA Nay, either tell me where thou hast been, or I will not open my lips so wide as a bristle may enter in way of thy excuse. My lady will hang thee for thy absence.

> **1-3 'You're in real trouble. Where have you been?'**

FESTE Let her hang me: he that is well hanged in this world needs to fear no colours.

> **4-5 'If you're dead you've got nothing to be scared of.'**

MARIA Make that good.

> **6 'Explain that.'**

FESTE He shall see none to fear.

MARIA A good lenten answer. I can tell thee where that saying was born, of, 'I fear no colours.'

> lenten answer: a weak joke

FESTE Where, good Mistress Mary?

MARIA In the wars; and that may you be bold to say in your foolery.

FESTE Well, God give them wisdom that have it; and those that are fools, let them use their talents.

> **13-14 'My fooling is a God-given gift, so let me use it.'**

MARIA Yet you will be hanged for being so long absent – or to be turned away: is not that as good as a hanging to you?

> **15-17 'You'll be hanged or sacked by Olivia for being away so long.'**

FESTE Many a good hanging prevents a bad marriage; and for turning away, let summer bear it out.

MARIA You are resolute then?

FESTE Not so neither, but I am resolved on two points –

> points: laces to hold gaskins up

MARIA That if one break, the other will hold, or if both break, your gaskins fall.

> gaskins: trousers

FESTE Apt, in good faith, very apt. Well, go thy way; if Sir Toby would leave drinking, thou wert as witty a piece of Eve's flesh as any in Illyria.

> **24-6 'If only Sir Toby would stop drinking, you'd be the best wife for him in Illyria.'**

MARIA Peace, you rogue, no more o' that. Here comes my lady: make your excuse wisely, you were best. *[Exit]*

> **28 'You'd better make your excuse wisely.'**

FESTE Wit, and't be thy will, put me into good fooling! Those wits that think they have thee do very oft prove fools, and I that am sure I lack thee may pass for a wise man. For what says Quinapalus? 'Better a witty fool than a foolish wit'.

> Quinapalus: name Feste makes up — he's pretending to be clever

Enter OLIVIA *and* ATTENDANTS, *with* MALVOLIO

God bless thee, lady.

OLIVIA Take the fool away.

FESTE Do you not hear, fellows? Take away the lady.

OLIVIA Go to, y'are a dry fool: I'll no more of you; besides, you grow dishonest.

> **37-8 'Come off it, you've run out of jokes. I don't want anything more to do with you. Besides, you're getting unreliable.'**

FESTE Two faults, madonna, that drink and good counsel will amend: for give the dry fool drink, then is the fool not dry; bid the dishonest man mend himself; if he mend, he is no longer dishonest; if he cannot, let the botcher mend him. Anything that's mended is but patched: virtue that transgresses is but patched with sin, and sin that amends is but patched with virtue. If that this simple syllogism will serve, so; if it will not, what remedy? As there is no true cuckold but calamity, so beauty's a flower. The lady bade take away the fool; therefore I say again, take her away.

> **39-40 'A drink and good advice will fix those two faults.'**
>
> **41-3 'Tell the dishonest man to mend himself — if he mends he's not dishonest anymore. If he can't improve he'll have to be patched.'**
>
> transgresses: goes wrong
>
> syllogism: formula
>
> cuckold: someone whose partner has been unfaithful
>
> bade: ordered

OLIVIA Sir, I bade them take away you.

FESTE Misprision in the highest degree! Lady, *cucullus non facit monachum*: that's as much to say as I wear not motley in my brain. Good madonna, give me leave to prove you a fool.

> *cucullus non facit monachum*: you're not a monk just because you wear the outfit
>
> **52-3 'I may wear fool's clothes, but inside I'm no fool'.**

OLIVIA Can you do it?

FESTE Dexteriously, good madonna.

> Dexteriously: brilliantly

OLIVIA Make your proof.

FESTE I must catechise you for it, madonna. Good my mouse of virtue, answer me.

> catechise: ask you questions

OLIVIA Well, sir, for want of other idleness, I'll bide your proof.

> **60-61 'As I have nothing better to do, I wait for you to prove it.'**

FESTE Good madonna, why mourn'st thou?

OLIVIA Good fool, for my brother's death.

FESTE I think his soul is in hell, madonna.

OLIVIA I know his soul is in heaven, fool.

FESTE The more fool, madonna, to mourn for your brother's soul being in heaven. Take away the fool, gentlemen.

OLIVIA What think you of this fool, Malvolio? Doth he not mend?

> **68-9 'Isn't he improving?'**

MALVOLIO Yes, and shall do, till the pangs of death shake him; infirmity, that decays the wise, doth ever make the better fool.

> **70-72 'He'll get better till he dies. The more feeble he gets the better he'll be at fooling.'**

FESTE God send you, sir, a speedy infirmity, for the better increasing your folly! Sir Toby will be sworn that I am no fox, but he will not pass his word for twopence that you are no fool.

> **74-6 'Toby wouldn't say I'm clever, but even if you paid him he wouldn't deny you're a fool.'**

OLIVIA How say you to that, Malvolio?

MALVOLIO I marvel your ladyship takes delight in such a barren rascal. I saw him put down the other day with an ordinary fool that has no more brain than a stone. Look you now, he's out of his guard already. Unless you laugh and minister occasion to him, he is gagged. I protest I take these wise men that crow so at these set kind of fools no better than the fools' zanies.

> **78-80 'I'm amazed you find him funny. I saw him the other day with a completely brainless fool.'**
>
> out of his guard: lost his concentration
>
> crow: fuss over
>
> **82-4 'Wise people who laugh at this sort of fool are no better than their assistants.'**

85-6 'Malvolio, you're so pompous. You take things too seriously.'

OLIVIA O you are sick of self-love, Malvolio, and taste with a distempered appetite. To be generous, guiltless, and of free disposition is to take those things for bird-bolts that you deem cannon bullets. There is no slander in an allowed fool though he do nothing but rail; nor no railing in a known discreet man though he do nothing but reprove.

make mountains out of molehills

god of liars

88-91 'He's not insulting you, even when he's ranting — nor does a wise man rant, even when he's criticising.'

FESTE Now Mercury endue thee with leasing, for thou speak'st well of fools!

Enter MARIA

92-3 'Let Mercury teach you to lie, as you speak kindly of fools.'

MARIA Madam, there is at the gate a young gentleman much desires to speak with you.

OLIVIA From the Count Orsino, is it?

MARIA I know not, madam; 'tis a fair young man and well attended.

with lots of servants

OLIVIA Who of my people hold him in delay?

MARIA Sir Toby, madam, your kinsman.

OLIVIA Fetch him off, I pray you; he speaks nothing but madman. Fie on him. *[Exit Maria]* Go you, Malvolio. If it be a suit from the count, I am sick, or not at home – what you will to dismiss it. *Exit Malvolio*
Now you see, sir, how your fooling grows old, and people dislike it.

103-4 'If he's come with a message of love from Orsino, make an excuse and send him away.'

FESTE Thou hast spoke for us, madonna, as if thy eldest son should be a fool: whose skull Jove cram with brains, for – here he comes –

107-8 'You stood up for me so well that you'd make a good mother for a fool.'

Enter SIR TOBY *[staggering]*

one of thy kin has a most weak *pia mater.*

110 'one of your relatives is a bit soft in the head.'

I'm a little bit tiddly... hic.

OLIVIA By mine honour, half drunk! What is he at the gate, cousin?

SIR TOBY A gentleman.

OLIVIA A gentleman! What gentleman?

SIR TOBY 'Tis a gentleman here – *[Hiccuping]* a plague o' these pickle herring! How now, sot?

drunken fool

FESTE Good Sir Toby –

OLIVIA Cousin, cousin, how have you come so early by this lethargy?

sleepiness

SIR TOBY Lechery! I defy lechery. There's one at the gate.

OLIVIA Ay, marry, what is he?

SIR TOBY Let him be the devil and he will, I care not: give me faith, say I. Well, it's all one. *Exit*

122-3 Don't worry — this doesn't make any sense. It's drunken ranting.

OLIVIA What's a drunken man like, fool?

FESTE Like a drowned man, a fool, and a madman: one draught above heat makes him a fool, the second mads him, and a third drowns him.

one drink over the limit

OLIVIA Go thou and seek the crowner, and let him sit o' my coz, for he's in the third degree of drink: he's drowned. Go look after him.

128-9 'Go and get the coroner, to do an inquest on my cousin — he's drunk so much he's drowned.'

FESTE He is but mad yet, madonna, and the fool shall look to the madman. *[Exit]*

131-2 'He's not drowned yet, just mad. I'll look after him.'

Enter MALVOLIO

MALVOLIO Madam, yond young fellow swears he will speak with you. I told him you were sick; he takes on him to understand so much and therefore comes to speak with you. I told him you were asleep; he seems to have a foreknowledge of that too, and therefore comes to speak with you. What is to be said to him, lady? He's fortified against any denial.

138-9 'Whatever I say he's got an excuse ready.'

OLIVIA Tell him he shall not speak with me.

MALVOLIO H'as been told so; and he says he'll stand at your door like a sheriff's post, and be the supporter to a bench, but he'll speak with you.

141-3 'He's not going anywhere, until he's allowed to speak to you.'

post to show where the sheriff lives

OLIVIA What kind o' man is he?

MALVOLIO Why, of mankind.

OLIVIA What manner of man?

MALVOLIO Of very ill manner: he'll speak with you, will you or no.

147-8 'He'll speak to you whether you like it or not.'

OLIVIA Of what personage and years is he?

149 'What does he look like and how old is he?'

MALVOLIO Not yet old enough for a man, nor young enough for a boy: as a squash is before 'tis a peascod, or a codling when 'tis almost an apple. 'Tis with him in standing water, between boy and man. He is very well-favoured and he speaks very shrewishly. One would think his mother's milk were scarce out of him.

unripe pea pod

unripe apple

153-5 'He's handsome and speaks in a high-pitched voice. You'd think he'd barely stopped breast-feeding.'

OLIVIA Let him approach. Call in my gentlewoman.

MALVOLIO Gentlewoman, my lady calls. *Exit*

Enter MARIA

OLIVIA Give me my veil; come throw it o'er my face. We'll once more hear Orsino's embassy.

Enter VIOLA

VIOLA The honourable lady of the house, which is she?

OLIVIA Speak to me; I shall answer for her. Your will?

VIOLA Most radiant, exquisite, and unmatchable beauty – I pray you tell me if this be the lady of the house, for I never saw her. I would be loath to cast away my speech: for besides that it is excellently well penned, I have taken great pains to con it. Good beauties, let me sustain no scorn; I am very comptible, even to the least

164-7 'I wouldn't want to waste my speech — it's well written and I've learnt it by heart. Don't make fun of me — I'm very sensitive.'

169 'Where are you from?'

170-72 'I have learned what I am going to say, and that's not part of it. Please give me at least some indication that you really are Olivia.'

174 'Are you an actor?'

175-6 'No, honestly not – though I admit I'm not quite who I seem.'

178 'Yes, unless I'm pretending to be me'.

179-81 'You <u>are</u> conning yourself; you're hanging on to something which you should be giving away. But that wasn't in my instructions.'

184-5 'I'll let you off the praise.'

likely to be false

188-9 'I only let you in to look at you, because I heard you were being cheeky at the gates.'

190-92 'I'm not feeling mad enough for this silly conversation.'

leave

deck-scrubber

stay

197-8 'You must have some terrible message to be so polite.'

199-200 'I'm not here to warn you of a quarrel, or to order you to be obedient.'

201 'There's as much peace in my words as there is business.'

204-6 'I was rude in reaction to my treatment. What I am and what I want are as secret as virginity.'

What is your text?

Erm... It's an Ace Book from CGP, miss.

sinister usage. rough treatment

OLIVIA Whence came you, sir?

VIOLA I can say little more than I have studied, and that question's out of my part. Good gentle one, give me modest assurance if you be the lady of the house, that I may proceed in my speech.

OLIVIA Are you a comedian?

VIOLA No, my profound heart; and yet, by the very fangs of malice, I swear, I am not that I play. Are you the lady of the house?

OLIVIA If I do not usurp myself, I am.

VIOLA Most certain, if you are she, you do usurp yourself: for what is yours to bestow is not yours to reserve. But this is from my commission. I will on with my speech in your praise, and then show you the heart of my message.

OLIVIA Come to what is important in't: I forgive you the praise.

VIOLA Alas, I took great pains to study it, and 'tis poetical.

OLIVIA It is the more like to be feigned; I pray you keep it in. I heard you were saucy at my gates, and allowed your approach rather to wonder at you than to hear you. If you be mad, be gone; if you have reason, be brief. 'Tis not that time of moon with me to make one in so skipping a dialogue.

MARIA Will you hoist sail, sir? Here lies your way.

VIOLA No, good swabber, I am to hull here a little longer. Some mollification for your giant, sweet lady! Tell me your mind, I am a messenger.

OLIVIA Sure you have some hideous matter to deliver, when the courtesy of it is so fearful. Speak your office.

VIOLA It alone concerns your ear. I bring no overture of war, no taxation of homage; I hold the olive in my hand; my words are as full of peace as matter.

OLIVIA Yet you began rudely. What are you? What would you?

VIOLA The rudeness that hath appeared in me I learned from my entertainment. What I am, and what I would, are as secret as maidenhead: to your ears, divinity; to any other's, profanation. blasphemy

OLIVIA Give us the place alone; we will hear this divinity. *[Exeunt Maria and Attendants]* Now, sir, what is your text?

VIOLA Most sweet lady –

OLIVIA A comfortable doctrine, and much may be said of it. Where lies your text?

VIOLA In Orsino's bosom.

OLIVIA In his bosom? In what chapter of his bosom? in the same style

VIOLA To answer by the method, in the first of his heart. lies

OLIVIA O! I have read it. It is heresy. Have you no more to say?

VIOLA Good madam, let me see your face.

OLIVIA Have you any commission from your lord to negotiate with my face? You are now out of your text, but we will draw the curtain and show you the picture. *[Unveiling]* Look you, sir, such a one I was this present. Is't not well done?

VIOLA Excellently done, if God did all.

OLIVIA 'Tis in grain, sir; 'twill endure wind and weather. the colour won't run

VIOLA 'Tis beauty truly blent, whose red and white blended
Nature's own sweet and cunning hand laid on.
Lady, you are the cruellest she alive,
If you will lead these graces to the grave,
And leave the world no copy.

OLIVIA O sir, I will not be so hard-hearted: I will give out divers schedules of my beauty. It shall be inventoried and every particle and utensil labelled to my will, as, *item,* two lips, indifferent red; *item,* two grey eyes, with lids to them; *item,* one neck, one chin, and so forth. Were you sent hither to praise me?

Two lips, indifferent red | Two Eyes, grey | One neck | One chin | Jumble Sale — everything 50p

VIOLA I see you what you are. You are too proud;
But if you were the devil, you are fair!
My lord and master loves you. O such love
Could be but recompensed, though you were crowned
The nonpareil of beauty.

OLIVIA How does he love me?

VIOLA With adorations, fertile tears,
With groans that thunder love, with sighs of fire.

OLIVIA Your lord does know my mind. I cannot love him.
Yet I suppose him virtuous, know him noble,
Of great estate, of fresh and stainless youth;
In voices well divulged, free, learned, and valiant,
And in dimension, and the shape of nature,
A gracious person. But yet I cannot love him.
He might have took his answer long ago.

VIOLA If I did love you in my master's flame,
With such a suff'ring, such a deadly life,
In your denial I would find no sense;
I would not understand it.

OLIVIA Why, what would you?

219-23 'Did Orsino ask you to talk to my face? You've changed the subject, but I'll show you my face. Look, it's a recent portrait. Isn't it well painted?'

228-30 'You're the cruellest woman alive if you die without leaving the world children, as a record of your beauty.'

238 'even if you were the devil I'd have to admit you're beautiful'

239-41 'Even if you were so beautiful that no one else's beauty came close to yours, it would only be fair repayment for Orsino's love.'

245-9 'I assume he's virtuous, know he's noble, wealthy, young, has a good reputation, is generous, educated, brave, and handsome.'

251-3 'If I loved you as passionately and painfully as Orsino, I wouldn't see the logic in your refusal.'

VIOLA Make me a willow cabin at your gate,
And call upon my soul within the house;
Write loyal cantons of contemnèd love,
And sing them loud even in the dead of night;
Hallow your name to the reverberate hills,
And make the babbling gossip of the air
Cry out 'Olivia!' O, you should not rest
Between the elements of air and earth
But you should pity me!

OLIVIA You might do much. What is your parentage?

VIOLA Above my fortunes, yet my state is well:
I am a gentleman.

OLIVIA Get you to your lord.
I cannot love him. Let him send no more –
Unless (perchance) you come to me again,
To tell me how he takes it. Fare you well.
I thank you for your pains. Spend this for me.

VIOLA I am no fee'd post, lady; keep your purse;
My master, not myself, lacks recompense.
Love make his heart of flint that you shall love,
And let your fervour like my master's be
Placed in contempt. Farewell, fair cruelty. *Exit*

OLIVIA 'What is your parentage?'
'Above my fortunes, yet my state is well:
I am a gentleman.' I'll be sworn thou art;
Thy tongue, thy face, thy limbs, actions, and spirit
Do give thee five-fold blazon. Not too fast! Soft, soft!
Unless the master were the man – How now?
Even so quickly may one catch the plague?
Methinks I feel this youth's perfections
With an invisible and subtle stealth
To creep in at mine eyes. Well, let it be.
What ho, Malvolio!

Enter MALVOLIO

MALVOLIO Here, madam, at your service.

OLIVIA Run after that same peevish messenger,
The county's man. He left this ring behind him,
Would I, or not. Tell him, I'll none of it.
Desire him not to flatter with his lord,
Nor hold him up with hopes; I am not for him.
If that the youth will come this way tomorrow,
I'll give him reasons for't. Hie thee, Malvolio!

MALVOLIO Madam, I will. *Exit*

OLIVIA I do I know not what, and fear to find
Mine eye too great a flatterer for my mind.
Fate, show thy force; ourselves we do not owe.
What is decreed must be; and be this so. *[Exit]*

257 'write faithful poems about my rejected love'

259 'shout your name in praise to the echoing hills'

261-3 'You would find no rest in this world until you took pity on me.'

264 'What sort of people were your parents?'

265 'Better off than I am now, but I'm doing OK'

paid messenger

273-5 'When you do fall in love, I hope his heart will be like flint so that your passion is ignored like my master's.'

a five part coat of arms

281-5 'Now if the boss was this chap — hang on, can you really fall in love so fast? I think I'm falling for him.'

This wasn't meant to happen...

287-8 'Run after that irritating messenger, Count Orsino's man.'

295-6 'I don't know what I'm doing. I'm afraid my eyes might be misleading my mind.'

own

298 'What fate decrees must happen; so let this happen.'

ACT 2 SCENE 5
Olivia's garden

Maria sets up the trick on Malvolio. Sir Toby, Fabian and Sir Andrew watch him fall for it.

Enter SIR TOBY, SIR ANDREW *and* FABIAN

SIR TOBY Come thy ways, Signior Fabian.

FABIAN Nay, I'll come. If I lose a scruple of this sport, let me be boiled to death with melancholy.

SIR TOBY Wouldst thou not be glad to have the niggardly rascally sheep-biter come by some notable shame?

FABIAN I would exult, man. You know he brought me out o' favour with my lady about a bear-baiting here.

SIR TOBY To anger him, we'll have the bear again; and we will fool him black and blue, shall we not, Sir Andrew?

SIR ANDREW And we do not, it is pity of our lives.

SIR TOBY Here comes the little villain.

Enter MARIA

How now, my metal of India?

MARIA Get ye all three into the box-tree. Malvolio's coming down this walk. He has been yonder i' the sun practising behaviour to his own shadow this half hour. Observe him, for the love of mockery, for I know this letter will make a contemplative idiot of him. Close, in the name of jesting! *[The men hide]* Lie thou there *[Drops a letter]*; for here comes the trout that must be caught with tickling. *Exit*

Enter MALVOLIO

MALVOLIO 'Tis but fortune; all is fortune. Maria once told me she did affect me, and I have heard herself come thus near, that should she fancy, it should be one of my complexion. Besides, she uses me with a more exalted respect than any one else that follows her. What should I think on't?

SIR TOBY Here's an overweening rogue!

FABIAN O peace! Contemplation makes a rare turkey-cock of him; how he jets under his advanced plumes!

SIR ANDREW 'Slight, I could so beat the rogue!

FABIAN Peace, I say!

MALVOLIO To be Count Malvolio!

SIR TOBY Ah, rogue!

SIR ANDREW Pistol him, pistol him!

FABIAN Peace, peace!

MALVOLIO There is example for't. The Lady of the Strachy married the yeoman of the wardrobe –

1 'Hurry up, Fabian.'

2-3 'I'm coming. I'd rather die of melancholy than miss this.'

4-5 'Wouldn't it be great to see that rotten Malvolio get seriously shown up?'

10 'If we didn't, we wouldn't deserve to live.'

precious (literally gold)

hide

caught by tickling his belly till he floats back into the tickler's hands

admire

colouring

24-5 'Besides, she treats me with more respect than any of her other servants.'

28-9 'Be quiet! What a turkey! Look at him strutting about with his feathers puffed out!'

Bang!

34 'Shoot him!'

36-7 'If I married Olivia, I wouldn't be the first servant to marry his Lady.'

shame on him

SIR ANDREW Fie on him, Jezebel!

FABIAN O peace! Now he's deeply in. Look how imagination blows him.

MALVOLIO Having been three months married to her, sitting in my state –

crossbow that fires stones

SIR TOBY O, for a stone-bow to hit him in the eye!

embroidered / **couch**

MALVOLIO Calling my officers about me, in my branched velvet gown, having come from a day-bed, where I have left Olivia sleeping –

SIR TOBY Fire and brimstone!

FABIAN O peace, peace!

49-52 'I would be very dignified. I would look gravely at everyone, to show I know my place, and they should know theirs. Then I'd send for Toby.'

MALVOLIO And then to have the humour of state; and after a demure travel of regard – telling them I know my place, as I would they should do theirs – to ask for my kinsman Toby –

SIR TOBY Bolts and shackles!

FABIAN O peace, peace, peace! Now, now!

57 He nearly says 'my steward's chain', then catches himself, and says 'some rich jewel'.

MALVOLIO Seven of my people, with an obedient start, make out for him. I frown the while, and perchance wind up my watch, or play with my – some rich jewel. Toby approaches; curtsies there to me –

SIR TOBY Shall this fellow live?

horses and carts

FABIAN Though our silence be drawn from us by cars, yet peace!

MALVOLIO I extend my hand to him thus, quenching my familiar smile with an austere regard of control –

SIR TOBY And does not 'Toby' take you a blow o' the lips then?

66-7 'Since I'm married to your niece, I have the right to say this –'

MALVOLIO Saying, 'Cousin Toby, my fortunes having cast me on your niece, give me this prerogative of speech –'

SIR TOBY What, what?

MALVOLIO 'You must amend your drunkenness.'

SIR TOBY Out, scab!

FABIAN Nay, patience, or we break the sinews of our plot.

MALVOLIO 'Besides, you waste the treasure of your time with a foolish knight –'

SIR ANDREW That's me, I warrant you.

MALVOLIO 'One Sir Andrew –'

77-8 'What have we got here?'

SIR ANDREW I knew 'twas I, for many do call me fool.

MALVOLIO *[Taking up the letter]* What employment have we here?

79 'Now the bird's near the trap.' Woodcocks were thought to be very stupid.

SIR TOBY Now is the woodcock near the gin.

80-81 'Let's hope he reads it out loud.'

FABIAN O peace, and the spirit of humours intimate reading aloud to him!

MALVOLIO By my life, this is my lady's hand: these be her very 'C's, her 'U's, and her 'T's, and thus makes she her great 'P's. It is, in contempt of question, her hand.

84 'It's definitely Olivia's handwriting.'

SIR ANDREW Her 'C's, her 'U's, and her 'T's: why that?

87-9 'This must be written by Olivia – it sounds like her, and it has the stamp she uses to seal her letters.'

MALVOLIO *[Reads]* 'To the unknown beloved, this, and my good wishes' – her very phrases! By your leave, wax. Soft! And the impressure her Lucrece, with which she uses to seal: 'tis my lady. To whom should this be? *[Opens the letter]*

FABIAN This wins him, liver and all.

MALVOLIO *[Reads]*
'Jove knows I love,
But who?
Lips, do not move:
No man must know.'

95-6 'The metre changes!'

'No man must know.' What follows? The numbers altered! 'No man must know'! If this should be thee, Malvolio!

badger

SIR TOBY Marry, hang thee, brock!

MALVOLIO *[Reads]*
'I may command where I adore,
But silence, like a Lucrece knife,
With bloodless stroke my heart doth gore;
M.O.A.I. doth sway my life.'

worthless

FABIAN A fustian riddle!

SIR TOBY Excellent wench, say I.

MALVOLIO 'M.O.A.I. doth sway my life.' Nay, but first let me see, let me see – let me see.

FABIAN What dish o' poison has she dressed him!

kestrel darts

SIR TOBY And with what wing the staniel checks at it!

110-13 'It's obvious to anyone of normal intelligence. There's nothing hard about this. But what does the arrangement of letters at the end mean?'

MALVOLIO 'I may command where I adore.' Why, she may command me: I serve her; she is my lady. Why, this is evident to any formal capacity. There is no obstruction in this, and the end – what should that alphabetical position portend? If I could make that resemble something in me – Softly! 'M.O.A.I.' –

115 'He's lost the trail.'

SIR TOBY O ay, make up that! He is now at a cold scent.

cobbler, but here it's a fox hound's name / **smelly**

FABIAN Sowter will cry upon't for all this, though it be as rank as a fox.

MALVOLIO 'M' – Malvolio. 'M' – why, that begins my name!

dog

FABIAN Did not I say he would work it out? The cur is excellent at faults.

122 'it doesn't make sense'

MALVOLIO 'M' – but then there is no consonancy in the

123 'makes less sense when you look closely'

125 'And the hangman's noose (O) will finish you off, I hope.'

beat with a club

128-130 'If you had eyes in the back of your head you'd see you were losing more than you're looking forward to.'

131-3 'This doesn't look as hopeful for me as it did before, but you can <u>make</u> it fit me'

135 'If you get this letter, think carefully.'

by birth

139-45 'Your fate is looking good. Embrace it body and soul. Practice for being what you're likely to become. Stop acting humbly. Antagonise a relation, be unfriendly to servants. Talk loudly about politics, get used to being noticed.'

with ribbons tied above and below the knee to hold up stockings

149-52 'I tell you — your fortune's made if you want it. If not, just stick to being a steward, a companion of servants and unworthy of good fortune.'

155 'This wouldn't be more obvious in broad daylight and open country.'

political

157-61 'I'll put down Sir Toby, I'll stop mixing with uncivilized people. I will be, to every last detail, the man described in this letter. I won't be fooled — it's obvious she loves me.'

165-6 'I'll stand apart and be proud'

sequel; that suffers under probation. 'A' should follow, but 'O' does.

FABIAN And 'O' shall end, I hope.

SIR TOBY Ay, or I'll cudgel him and make him cry 'O'!

MALVOLIO And then 'I' comes behind.

FABIAN Ay, and you had any eye behind you, you might see more detraction at your heels than fortunes before you.

MALVOLIO 'M.O.A.I.' This simulation is not as the former, and yet, to crush this a little, it would bow to me, for every one of these letters are in my name. Soft, here follows prose.

[Reads] 'If this fall into thy hand, revolve. In my stars I am above thee, but be not afraid of greatness. Some are born great, some achieve greatness, and some have greatness thrust upon 'em. Thy fates open their hands; let thy blood and spirit embrace them, and, to inure thyself to what thou art like to be, cast thy humble slough and appear fresh. Be opposite with a kinsman, surly with servants; let thy tongue tang arguments of state; put thy self into the trick of singularity. She thus advises thee that sighs for thee. Remember who commended thy yellow stockings and wished to see thee ever cross-gartered: I say, remember. Go to, thou art made if thou desir'st to be so; if not, let me see thee a steward still, the fellow of servants, and not worthy to touch Fortune's fingers. Farewell. She that would alter services with thee,

The Fortunate-Unhappy.'

roles

Daylight and champain discovers not more! This is open. I will be proud, I will read politic authors, I will baffle Sir Toby, I will wash off gross acquaintance, I will be point-device, the very man. I do not now fool myself to let imagination jade me; for every reason excites to this, that my lady loves me. She did commend my yellow stockings of late, she did praise my leg being cross-gartered; and in this she manifests herself to my love, and with a kind of injunction drives me to these habits of her liking. I thank my stars, I am happy. I will be strange, stout, in yellow stockings, and cross-gartered, even with the swiftness of putting on. Jove and my stars be praised! – Here is yet a postscript. *[Reads]* 'Thou canst not choose but know who I am. If thou entertain'st my love, let it appear in thy smiling; thy smiles become thee well. Therefore in my presence still smile, dear my sweet, I prithee.' Jove, I thank thee. I will smile; I will do everything that thou wilt have me.

Exit

FABIAN I will not give my part of this sport for a pension of thousands to be paid from the Sophy.

SIR TOBY I could marry this wench for this device –

SIR ANDREW So could I, too.

SIR TOBY And ask no other dowry with her but such another jest.

SIR ANDREW Nor I neither.

FABIAN Here comes my noble gull-catcher.

Enter MARIA

SIR TOBY Wilt thou set thy foot o' my neck?

SIR ANDREW Or o' mine either?

SIR TOBY Shall I play my freedom at tray-trip and become thy bond-slave?

SIR ANDREW I' faith, or I either?

SIR TOBY Why, thou hast put him in such a dream that when the image of it leaves him, he must run mad.

MARIA Nay, but say true, does it work upon him?

SIR TOBY Like aqua-vitae with a midwife.

MARIA If you will then see the fruits of the sport, mark his first approach before my lady. He will come to her in yellow stockings, and 'tis a colour she abhors, and cross-gartered, a fashion she detests; and he will smile upon her, which will now be so unsuitable to her disposition, being addicted to a melancholy as she is, that it cannot but turn him into a notable contempt. If you will see it, follow me.

SIR TOBY To the gates of Tartar, thou most excellent devil of wit!

SIR ANDREW I'll make one too. *Exeunt*

Roman chief of the gods

170-72 'If you are glad of my love, smile when you're with me — your smiles suit you.'

ruler of Persia

178 For the rest of this page Sir Andrew just echoes what Toby says — once again making himself sound foolish.

catcher of fools

185-6 'Shall I gamble my freedom and become your slave?'

alcoholic spirit

can't stand

195-9 'He'll smile at her, but she's so addicted to sadness now that she'll think he's a disgrace.'

200-201 'To the gates of hell, you fiend.'

Yup - I'm sexy.

Viola comes to see Olivia. Olivia's really fallen for Cesario, and Viola has to try and put Olivia off without revealing her disguise.

ACT 3 SCENE 1
Olivia's garden

small drum

Enter VIOLA *and* FESTE, *playing on a pipe and tabor*

VIOLA Save thee, friend, and thy music! Dost thou live by thy tabor?

FESTE No, sir, I live by the church.

VIOLA Art thou a churchman?

FESTE No such matter, sir. I do live by the church; for I do live at my house, and my house doth stand by the church.

4 Viola's being playful here — she knows Feste's not a priest because he's wearing a fool's outfit.

sleeps with

is supported by

VIOLA So thou mayst say the king lies by a beggar, if a beggar dwell near him; or the church stands by thy tabor if thy tabor stand by the church.

FESTE You have said, sir. To see this age! A sentence is but a cheveril glove to a good wit – how quickly the wrong side may be turned outward!

10-11 'A clever person can turn a sentence inside out like a kid glove.'

VIOLA Nay, that's certain: they that dally nicely with words may quickly make them wanton.

13-14 'People who mess around with words make them loose.'

FESTE I would therefore my sister had had no name, sir.

VIOLA Why, man?

FESTE Why, sir, her name's a word, and to dally with that word might make my sister wanton; but, indeed, words are very rascals, since bonds disgraced them.

VIOLA Thy reason, man?

FESTE Truth, sir, I can yield you none without words, and words are grown so false, I am loath to prove reason with them.

21-3 'You can't tell the truth without words, but words are so flexible that I don't think I can be logical with them.'

VIOLA I warrant thou art a merry fellow and car'st for nothing.

FESTE Not so, sir, I do care for something; but in my conscience, sir, I do not care for you: if that be to care for nothing, I would it would make you invisible.

VIOLA Art not thou the Lady Olivia's fool?

FESTE No, indeed, sir. The Lady Olivia has no folly. She will keep no fool, sir, till she be married, and fools are as like husbands as pilchards are to herrings – the husband's the bigger. I am indeed not her fool but her corrupter of words.

29-32 'Olivia won't have a fool till she gets married. Fools and husbands are like pilchards and herrings — husbands are bigger.'

lately

VIOLA I saw thee late at the Count Orsino's.

FESTE Foolery, sir, does walk about the orb like the sun; it shines everywhere. I would be sorry, sir, but the fool should be as oft with your master as with my mistress: I think I saw your wisdom there.

planet

VIOLA Nay, and thou pass upon me, I'll no more with thee. Hold, there's expenses for thee. *[Gives a coin]*

FESTE Now Jove, in his next commodity of hair, send thee a beard!

hand-out

VIOLA By my troth, I'll tell thee, I am almost sick for one – *[Aside]* though I would not have it grow on my chin. Is thy lady within?

FESTE Would not a pair of these have bred, sir?

VIOLA Yes, being kept together and put to use.

FESTE I would play Lord Pandarus of Phrygia, sir, to bring a Cressida to this Troilus.

In the story of Troilus and Cressida, Lord Pandarus is their go-between.

48-9 'I'd be a go-between if you gave me one more coin.' Feste could mean he's going to matchmake the two coins, or Cesario and Olivia.

VIOLA I understand you sir; 'tis well begged. *[Gives another coin]*

FESTE The matter, I hope, is not great, sir – begging but a beggar: Cressida was a beggar. My lady is within, sir. I will construe to them whence you come; who you are, and what you would, are out of my welkin – I might say 'element', but the word is overworn.

52-4 'I'll explain to them that you're from Orsino's. Who you are and what you want is none of my business.'

VIOLA This fellow is wise enough to play the fool,
And to do that well craves a kind of wit;
He must observe their mood on whom he jests,
The quality of persons, and the time;
Not, like the haggard, check at every feather
That comes before his eye. This is a practice,
As full of labour as a wise man's art:
For folly that he wisely shows is fit;
But wise men, folly-fallen, quite taint their wit.

56-9 'This bloke's clever enough to be a fool; playing the fool does take brains of a sort. You have to think about the audience's mood, what sort of people they are, and the occasion.'

untrained hawk

snap at

61-4 'It's as hard as the jobs wise men do. When he's foolish it's on purpose. When wise men are foolish you wonder how clever they really are.'

Enter SIR TOBY *and* SIR ANDREW

SIR TOBY Save you, gentleman.

VIOLA And you, sir.

SIR ANDREW *Dieu vous garde, monsieur.*

67 'God keep you, sir.'

VIOLA *Et vous aussi; votre serviteur.*

68 'And you too; your servant.'

SIR ANDREW I hope, sir, you are, and I am yours.

SIR TOBY Will you encounter the house? My niece is desirous you should enter, if your trade be to her.

enter

VIOLA I am bound to your niece, sir; I mean, she is the list of my voyage.

destination

SIR TOBY Taste your legs, sir; put them to motion.

VIOLA My legs do better understand me, sir, than I understand what you mean by bidding me taste my legs.

stand under

Yuk!

SIR TOBY I mean, to go, sir, to enter.

VIOLA I will answer you with gait and entrance – but we are prevented.

78-9 'I will take steps and enter — but we can't go in (here comes Olivia).'

Enter OLIVIA *and* GENTLEWOMAN [MARIA]

Most excellent accomplished lady, the heavens rain

odours on you!
SIR ANDREW That youth's a rare courtier – 'rain odours' – well.
VIOLA My matter hath no voice, lady, but to your own most pregnant and vouchsafed ear.
SIR ANDREW 'Odours' 'pregnant', and 'vouchsafed': I'll get 'em all three all ready.
OLIVIA Let the garden door be shut, and leave me to my hearing. *[Exeunt Sir Toby, Sir Andrew, and Maria]*
Give me your hand, sir.
VIOLA My duty, madam, and most humble service.
OLIVIA What is your name?
VIOLA Cesario is your servant's name, fair princess.
OLIVIA My servant, sir? 'Twas never merry world
Since lowly feigning was called compliment.
Y'are servant to the Count Orsino, youth.
VIOLA And he is yours, and his must needs be yours:
Your servant's servant is your servant, madam.
OLIVIA For him, I think not on him; for his thoughts,
Would they were blanks, rather than filled with me!
VIOLA Madam, I come to whet your gentle thoughts
On his behalf.
OLIVIA O by your leave, I pray you!
I bade you never speak again of him;
But would you undertake another suit
I had rather hear you to solicit that,
Than music from the spheres.
VIOLA Dear lady –
OLIVIA Give me leave, beseech you. I did send,
After the last enchantment you did here,
A ring in chase of you. So did I abuse
Myself, my servant, and, I fear me, you.
Under your hard construction must I sit,
To force that on you in a shameful cunning
Which you knew none of yours. What might you think?
Have you not set mine honour at the stake,
And baited it with all th' unmuzzled thoughts
That tyrannous heart can think? To one of your receiving
Enough is shown; a cypress, not a bosom,
Hides my heart: so, let me hear you speak.
VIOLA I pity you.
OLIVIA That's a degree to love.
VIOLA No, not a grise; for 'tis a vulgar proof
That very oft we pity enemies.
OLIVIA Why then, methinks 'tis time to smile again.
O world, how apt the poor are to be proud!
If one should be a prey, how much the better
To fall before the lion than the wolf!
[Clock strikes]
The clock upbraids me with the waste of time.
Be not afraid, good youth; I will not have you –
And yet when wit and youth is come to harvest,
Your wife is like to reap a proper man.
There lies your way, due west.
VIOLA Then westward ho!
Grace and good disposition attend your ladyship!
You'll nothing, madam, to my lord by me?
OLIVIA Stay!
I prithee tell me what thou think'st of me.
VIOLA That you do think you are not what you are.
OLIVIA If I think so, I think the same of you.
VIOLA Then think you right: I am not what I am.
OLIVIA I would you were as I would have you be.
VIOLA Would it be better, madam, than I am?
I wish it might, for now I am your fool.
OLIVIA *[Aside]* O, what a deal of scorn looks beautiful
In the contempt and anger of his lip!
A murderous guilt shows not itself more soon,
Than love that would seem hid. Lovers' night is noon.
Cesario, by the roses of the spring,
By maidhood, honour, truth, and everything,
I love thee so that, maugre all thy pride,
Nor wit nor reason can my passion hide.
Do not extort thy reasons from this clause,
For that I woo, thou therefore hast no cause;
But rather reason thus with reason fetter:
Love sought is good, but giv'n unsought is better.
VIOLA By innocence I swear, and by my youth,
I have one heart, one bosom, and one truth,
And that no woman has; nor never none
Shall mistress be of it, save I alone.
And so, adieu, good madam; never more
Will I my master's tears to you deplore.
OLIVIA Yet come again: for thou perhaps mayst move
That heart which now abhors to like his love. *[Exeunt]*

---

sweet fragrances

outstanding

84-5 'My message is only for your ready and willing ear.'

86-7 'I'll make a note of those words.'

Mellifluous
Pregnant
Vouchsaife
~~Oders~~ odors

Andrew's book of nifty words

pretending to be respectful

99-100 'I don't think about Orsino, and I'd rather he had no thoughts at all than thought about me!'

sharpen, make keener

104-6 'If you would flirt for someone else, I'd rather listen to you than to the music of heaven.'

spell you cast

111-13 'You must think badly of me for forcing you to accept the ring (which you knew wasn't yours) in such a devious way.'

114-18 'Haven't you ripped my honour to shreds in your thoughts, like a dog at a bear-baiting? I've said enough, I'm going to hide my feelings. It's your turn to speak.'

120-21 'Not at all — it's common knowledge that people often pity their enemies.'

123 'Those who have nothing can still be proud!'

124-5 'Better to be the victim of a noble lion than of a hungry wolf.'

tells me off for

128-9 'When you have grown to maturity, your wife will harvest a decent man.'

135 'You think you are something you are not.'

143-4 'It's even harder to hide love than it is to hide a guilty conscience. Even when lovers are being secretive it's obvious what they're up to.'

despite

149-52 'Don't think that because I'm wooing you, you shouldn't be interested in me. It's good to be given love when you've asked for it, but it's better to be loved when you didn't expect it.'

Eek - I'd really better be going now.

Olivia calls for Malvolio who behaves strangely. Olivia leaves Maria and Sir Toby to look after him. Sir Andrew is jealous of Olivia's attention to Viola, and Sir Toby persuades him to start a fight.

ACT 3 SCENE 4
Olivia's garden

Enter OLIVIA *followed by* MARIA

OLIVIA *[Aside]* I have sent after him; he says he'll come –
How shall I feast him? What bestow of him?
For youth is bought more oft than begged or borrowed.
I speak too loud –
Where's Malvolio? He is sad and civil,
And suits well for a servant with my fortunes.
Where is Malvolio?

2-3 'How will I entertain him? What will I give him? Young people are more impressed by presents than begging and pleading.'

5-6 'He's serious and polite, and the right kind of servant for someone like me.'

MARIA He's coming, madam, but in very strange manner. He is sure possessed, madam.

OLIVIA Why, what's the matter? Does he rave?

MARIA No, madam, he does nothing but smile. Your ladyship were best to have some guard about you, if he come, for sure the man is tainted in's wits.

be on your guard

OLIVIA Go call him hither. *[Exit Maria]* I am as mad as he
If sad and merry madness equal be.

Enter MARIA *with* MALVOLIO

How now, Malvolio?

MALVOLIO Sweet lady, ho, ho!

OLIVIA Smil'st thou? I sent for thee upon a sad occasion.

MALVOLIO Sad, lady? I could be sad. This does make some obstruction in the blood, this cross-gartering, but what of that? If it please the eye of one, it is with me as the very true sonnet is: 'Please one, and please all.'

I can't feel my feet - this had better be worth it.

19-22 'This cross-gartering's cutting off my circulation, but so what? If you're happy I'm happy.'

OLIVIA Why, how dost thou, man? What is the matter with thee?

MALVOLIO Not black in my mind, though yellow in my legs. It did come to his hands, and commands shall be executed. I think we do know the sweet Roman hand.

25-7 'Someone found the you-know-what, and the orders will be obeyed. I know that lovely handwriting.'

OLIVIA Wilt thou go to bed, Malvolio?

MALVOLIO To bed? Ay, sweetheart, and I'll come to thee.

OLIVIA God comfort thee! Why dost thou smile so and kiss thy hand so oft?

MARIA How do you, Malvolio?

MALVOLIO At your request! Yes, nightingales answer daws!

33 'Nightingales, which are noble birds, will answer ordinary jackdaws.'

MARIA Why appear you with this ridiculous boldness before my lady?

MALVOLIO 'Be not afraid of greatness': 'twas well writ.

OLIVIA What meanest thou by that, Malvolio?

MALVOLIO 'Some are born great –'

OLIVIA Ha?

MALVOLIO 'Some achieve greatness –'

OLIVIA What say'st thou?

MALVOLIO 'And some have greatness thrust upon them'

OLIVIA Heaven restore thee!

MALVOLIO 'Remember who commended thy yellow stockings –'

OLIVIA Thy yellow stockings?

MALVOLIO 'And wished to see thee cross-gartered.'

OLIVIA Cross-gartered?

MALVOLIO 'Go to, thou art made, if thou desir'st to be so –'

OLIVIA Am I made?

MALVOLIO 'If not, let me see thee a servant still.'

OLIVIA Why, this is very midsummer madness.

36-51 Malvolio's quoting from the letter Maria wrote.

I think I'm going mad...wibble...

It was believed people were more likely to go mad in midsummer.

Enter SERVANT

SERVANT Madam, the young gentleman of the Count Orsino's is returned; I could hardly entreat him back. He attends your ladyship's pleasure.

persuade him to come back

OLIVIA I'll come to him. *[Exit Servant]* Good Maria, let this fellow be looked to. Where's my cousin Toby? Let some of my people have a special care of him; I would not have him miscarry for the half of my dowry.

come to any harm

[Exeunt Olivia and Maria]

MALVOLIO O ho! Do you come near me now? No worse man than Sir Toby to look to me! This concurs directly with the letter: she sends him on purpose that I may appear stubborn to him; for she incites me to that in the letter. 'Cast thy humble slough,' says she; 'be opposite with a kinsman, surly with servants, let thy tongue tang with arguments of state, put thyself into the trick of singularity,' and consequently sets down the manner how: as a sad face, a reverend carriage, a slow tongue, in the habit of some sir of note, and so forth. I have limed her, but it is Jove's doing, and Jove make me thankful! And when she went away now, 'Let this fellow be looked to' – 'fellow'! Not Malvolio, nor after my degree, but 'fellow.' Why, everything adheres together, that no dram of a scruple, no scruple of a scruple, no obstacle, no incredulous or unsafe circumstance – what can be said? Nothing that can be can come between me and the full prospect of my hopes. Well, Jove, not I, is the doer of this, and he is to be thanked!

agrees exactly

dignified bearing

69 'I've caught her like a bird in a trap.'

in keeping with my status as a servant

75-6 'There's nothing that can possibly come between me and what I hope for.'

Enter SIR TOBY, FABIAN, *and* MARIA

SIR TOBY Which way is he, in the name of sanctity? If all the devils of hell be drawn in little, and Legion himself possessed him, yet I'll speak to him.

78-80 'Even if he's possessed by all the devils in hell, I won't be stopped from speaking to him.'

83-4 **'Get away! I won't be needing you. Leave me in peace!' Malvolio's talking to the others like they were his servants.**

look after him

93-4 **'Look! If you say bad things about the devil he gets upset! I pray to God he hasn't had a spell cast on him.'**

95 **'Take a urine sample to the wise woman — she'll know if he's been bewitched.'**

100-101 **'Calm down, you're upsetting him. Leave me alone with him.'**

pretty bird

chicken

chickabiddy

107-8 **'You can't fool around with the devil.'**

filthy coalman

114-16 **'Go hang yourselves! You are lazy, worthless sorts; I'm a cut above you lot. You'll see.'**

118-19 **'If this was a play, I'd say it was completely unrealistic.'**

120-21 **'He's completely fallen for the trick.'**

122 **'Follow him, quick, in case he realises what's going on when he has a moment to himself.'**

FABIAN Here he is, here he is. How is't with you, sir?

SIR TOBY How is't with you, man?

MALVOLIO Go off, I discard you. Let me enjoy my private. Go off!

MARIA Lo, how hollow the fiend speaks within him! Did not I tell you? Sir Toby, my lady prays you to have a care of him.

MALVOLIO Ah ha! Does she so?

SIR TOBY Go to, go to; peace, peace! We must deal gently with him. Let me alone. How do you, Malvolio? How is't with you? What, man, defy the devil! Consider, he's an enemy to mankind.

MALVOLIO Do you know what you say?

MARIA La you! And you speak ill of the devil, how he takes it at heart! Pray God he be not bewitched!

FABIAN Carry his water to th' wise woman.

MARIA Marry, and it shall be done tomorrow morning if I live. My lady would not lose him for more than I'll say.

MALVOLIO How now, mistress?

MARIA O Lord!

SIR TOBY Prithee, hold thy peace; this is not the way. Do you not see you move him? Let me alone with him.

FABIAN No way but gentleness; gently, gently: the fiend is rough, and will not be roughly used.

SIR TOBY Why, how now, my bawcock? How dost thou, chuck?

MALVOLIO Sir!

SIR TOBY Ay, biddy, come with me. What, man, 'tis not for gravity to play at cherry-pit with Satan. Hang him, foul collier!

MARIA Get him to say his prayers, good Sir Toby, get him to pray.

MALVOLIO My prayers, minx!

MARIA No, I warrant you, he will not hear of godliness.

MALVOLIO Go hang yourselves all! You are idle, shallow things; I am not of your element. You shall know more hereafter. *Exit*

SIR TOBY Is't possible?

FABIAN If this were played upon a stage now, I could condemn it as an improbable fiction.

SIR TOBY His very genius hath taken the infection of the device, man.

MARIA Nay, pursue him now, lest the device take air and taint.

FABIAN Why, we shall make him mad indeed.

MARIA The house will be the quieter.

SIR TOBY Come, we'll have him in a dark room and bound. My niece is already in the belief that he's mad. We may carry it thus for our pleasure, and his penance, till our very pastime, tired out of breath, prompt us to have mercy on him; at which time we will bring the device to the bar and crown thee for a finder of madmen. But see, but see!

Enter SIR ANDREW

FABIAN More matter for a May morning!

SIR ANDREW Here's the challenge; read it. I warrant there's vinegar and pepper in't.

FABIAN Is't so saucy?

SIR ANDREW Ay, is't. I warrant him; do but read.

SIR TOBY Give me. *[Reads]* 'Youth, whatsoever thou art, thou art but a scurvy fellow.'

FABIAN Good, and valiant.

SIR TOBY *[Reads]* 'Wonder not, nor admire not in thy mind, why I do call thee so, for I will show thee no reason for't.'

FABIAN A good note! That keeps you from the blow of the law.

SIR TOBY *[Reads]* 'Thou com'st to the Lady Olivia, and in my sight she uses thee kindly. But thou liest in thy throat. That is not the matter I challenge thee for.'

FABIAN Very brief, and to exceeding good sense *[Aside]* – less.

SIR TOBY *[Reads]* 'I will waylay thee going home, where if it be thy chance to kill me –'

FABIAN Good.

SIR TOBY *[Reads]* 'Thou killest me like a rogue and a villain.'

FABIAN Still you keep o' th' windy side of the law. Good.

SIR TOBY *[Reads]* 'Fare thee well, and God have mercy upon one of our souls! He may have mercy upon mine, but my hope is better, and so look to thyself. Thy friend, as thou usest him, and thy sworn enemy,

Andrew Aguecheek.'

If this letter move him not, his legs cannot. I'll give't him.

MARIA You may have very fit occasion for't; he is now in some commerce with my lady and will by and by depart.

SIR TOBY Go, Sir Andrew, scout me for him at the corner of the orchard like a bum-baily. So soon as ever thou seest him, draw, and as thou draw'st, swear horrible; for it comes to pass oft that a terrible oath, with a swaggering accent sharply twanged off, gives manhood more approbation than ever proof itself would have earned him. Away!

SIR ANDREW Nay, let me alone for swearing. *Exit*

125 **'We'll tie him up and put him in a darkened room.'**

126-30 **'We'll carry on enjoying ourselves, and punishing him, until the trick runs out of steam, and we feel sorry for him. Then we'll bring it all out into the open.'**

131 **'More loopiness!'**

invitation to fight a duel

spicy

wretched individual

139-40 **'Don't question why I call you that. I'll give you no reason.'**

141-2 **'That'll keep you out of trouble with the law.'**

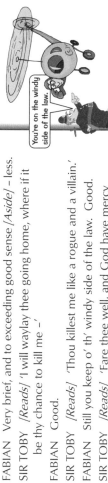

You're on the windy side of the law.

157 **'If that doesn't get him going then nothing will.'**

158-9 **'The right moment's coming up — he's talking to Olivia and he'll be off soon.'**

bailiff

Bailiffs sneak up on you from *behind*.

162-5 **'often a well-delivered curse makes you look more manly than actual manly behaviour.'**

170-72 'This letter's so badly written it won't scare the young man — he'll see it's from a blockhead.'

173-6 'I'll make out Andrew's a real he-man. The lad'll get a really terrible picture of him.'

SIR TOBY Now will not I deliver his letter; for the behaviour of the young gentleman gives him out to be of good capacity and breeding; his employment between his lord and my niece confirms no less. Therefore this letter, being so excellently ignorant, will breed no terror in the youth; he will find it comes from a clodpole. But, sir, I will deliver his challenge by word of mouth, set upon Aguecheek a notable report of valour, and drive the gentleman (as I know his youth will aptly receive it) into a most hideous opinion of his rage, skill, fury, and impetuosity. This will so fright them both that they will kill one another by the look, like cockatrices.

monstrous snakes that can kill with a stare

FABIAN Here he comes with your niece; give them way till he take leave and presently after him.

Enter OLIVIA *and* VIOLA

SIR TOBY I will meditate the while upon some horrid message for a challenge. *[Exeunt Sir Toby, Fabian & Maria]*

181-2 'I'll make up a really scary challenge.'

OLIVIA I have said too much unto a heart of stone,
And laid mine honour too unchary out;
There's something in me that reproves my fault,
But such a headstrong potent fault it is,
That it but mocks reproof.

188-9 'Orsino's as unhappy as you are.'

VIOLA With the same 'haviour that your passion bears
Goes on my master's griefs.

193-4 'Ask me for something. I'll give you anything, so long as I can give it, but keep my honour.'

OLIVIA Here, wear this jewel for me; 'tis my picture.
Refuse it not; it hath no tongue to vex you.
And, I beseech you, come again tomorrow.
What shall you ask of me that I'll deny,
That honour, saved, may upon asking give?

196-7 'It wouldn't be honourable to give him something I've already given to you.'

VIOLA Nothing but this – your true love for my master.

OLIVIA How with mine honour may I give him that
Which I have given to you?

VIOLA I will acquit you.

199 'I'd follow a friend like you anywhere — even to hell.'

OLIVIA Well, come again tomorrow. Fare thee well.
A friend like thee might bear my soul to hell. *[Exit]*

Enter SIR TOBY *and* FABIAN

SIR TOBY Gentleman, God save thee.

202 'Defend yourself however you can.'

VIOLA And you, sir.

204-6 'Your attacker is waiting in the orchard, full of venom. Unsheath your sword, prepare yourself quickly...'

SIR TOBY That defence thou hast, betake thee to't. Of what nature the wrongs are thou hast done him, I know not; but thy interceptor, full of despite, bloody as the hunter, attends thee at the orchard-end. Dismount thy tuck, be yare in thy preparation, for thy assailant is quick, skilful, and deadly.

209-10 'I never did anything to anyone.'

VIOLA You mistake, sir. I am sure no man hath any quarrel to me. My remembrance is very free and clear from any image of offence done to any man.

211-12 'if you value your life at all'

213-14 'your opponent's got everything that youth, strength, skill and anger can give a man.'

SIR TOBY You'll find it otherwise, I assure you. Therefore, if you hold your life at any price, betake you to your guard; for your opposite hath in him what youth, strength, skill, and wrath can furnish man withal.

VIOLA I pray you, sir, what is he?

216-17 'He was made knight with an unused sword, for work indoors, not on the battlefield'

218-21 'He's killed three people, and he's so angry now, that only death and the tomb will satisfy him.'

SIR TOBY He is knight, dubbed with unhatched rapier, and on carpet consideration, but he is a devil in private brawl. Souls and bodies hath he divorced three, and his incensement at this moment is so implacable that satisfaction can be none but by pangs of death and sepulchre. Hob-nob is his word: give't or take't.

have or don't have (your life)

224-5 'men who start fights with others to test their bravery; I suppose he's one of those.'

VIOLA I will return again into the house and desire some conduct of the lady. I am no fighter. I have heard of some kind of men that put quarrels purposely on others to taste their valour; belike this is a man of that quirk.

231-2 'you've got to get involved, or give up wearing a sword altogether.'

Only gentlemen wore swords. Toby's saying Viola's not behaving like a gentleman.

SIR TOBY Sir, no. His indignation derives itself out of a very competent injury; therefore get you on and give him his desire. Back you shall not to the house, unless you undertake that with me which with as much safety you might answer him; therefore on, or strip your sword stark naked; for meddle you must, that's certain, or forswear to wear iron about you.

VIOLA This is as uncivil as strange. I beseech you, do me this courteous office as to know of the knight what my offence to him is. It is something of my negligence, nothing of my purpose.

SIR TOBY I will do so. Signior Fabian, stay you by this gentleman till my return. *Exit Sir Toby*

240-41 'I know the knight's angry enough to fight to the death, but nothing more.'

VIOLA Pray you, sir, do you know of this matter?

FABIAN I know the knight is incensed against you, even to a mortal arbitrement, but nothing of the circumstance more.

VIOLA I beseech you, what manner of man is he?

243-4 'To look at him you'd never think he was a brave man.'

FABIAN Nothing of that wonderful promise, to read him by his form, as you are like to find him in the proof of his valour. He is indeed, sir, the most skilful, bloody, and fatal opposite that you could possibly have found in any part of Illyria. Will you walk towards him? I will make your peace with him if I can.

249-51 'I'd always rather negotiate than fight. I don't care who knows it.'

VIOLA I shall be much bound to you for't. I am one that had rather go with sir priest than sir knight. I care not who knows so much of my mettle. *Exeunt*

Enter SIR TOBY *and* SIR ANDREW

SIR TOBY Why, man, he's a very devil; I have not seen such a

253-6 'I had a fencing bout with him — you can't avoid his thrusts.'

female warrior

firago. I had a pass with him, rapier, scabbard, and all, and he gives me the stuck-in with such a mortal motion that it is inevitable; and on the answer, he pays you as surely as your feet hits the ground they step on. They say he has been fencer to the Sophy.

fencing instructor to the ruler of Persia

SIR ANDREW Pox on't. I'll not meddle with him.

SIR TOBY Ay, but he will not now be pacified. Fabian can scarce hold him yonder.

261-3 'Damn, if I'd thought he was brave and a good fencer, I'd never have challenged him.'

SIR ANDREW Plague on't, and I thought he had been valiant, and so cunning in fence, I'd have seen him damned ere I'd have challenged him. Let him let the matter slip, and I'll give him my horse, grey Capilet.

suggestion

SIR TOBY I'll make the motion. Stand here, make a good show on't. This shall end without the perdition of souls. *[Aside]* Marry, I'll ride your horse as well as I ride you.

loss

Enter FABIAN *and* VIOLA

[To Fabian] I have his horse to take up the quarrel. I have persuaded him the youth's a devil.

terrified

FABIAN He is as horribly conceited of him and pants and looks pale, as if a bear were at his heels.

No! Start again
I wasn't ready.

SIR TOBY *[To Viola]* There's no remedy, sir. He will fight with you for's oath sake. Marry, he hath better bethought him of his quarrel, and he finds that now scarce to be worth talking of. Therefore, draw for the supportance of his vow. He protests he will not hurt you.

honour's

VIOLA *[Aside]* Pray God defend me! A little thing would make me tell them how much I lack of a man.

FABIAN Give ground if you see him furious.

SIR TOBY Come, Sir Andrew, there's no remedy: the gentleman will for his honour's sake have one bout with you; he cannot by the duello avoid it, but he has promised me, as he is a gentleman and a soldier, he will not hurt you. Come on, to't.

duelling rules

SIR ANDREW Pray God he keep his oath!

VIOLA I do assure you, 'tis against my will. *[They draw]*

Enter ANTONIO

ANTONIO *[Drawing]* Put up your sword! If this young gentleman
Have done offence, I take the fault on me;
If you offend him, I for him defy you.

SIR TOBY You, sir? Why, what are you?

ANTONIO One, sir, that for his love dares yet do more
Than you have heard him brag to you he will.

293 'If you're going to stick your nose in, I'll fight you.'

SIR TOBY Nay, if you be an undertaker, I am for you. *[Draws]*

Enter OFFICERS

FABIAN O good Sir Toby, hold! Here comes the officers.

SIR TOBY *[To Antonio]* I'll be with you anon.

later

VIOLA *[To Sir Andrew]* Pray, sir, put your sword up, if you please.

SIR ANDREW Marry, will I, sir; and for that I promised you, I'll be as good as my word. He will bear you easily and reins well.

299-300 Sir Andrew's talking about his horse.

1ST OFFICER This is the man; do thy office.

2ND OFFICER Antonio, I arrest thee at the suit
Of Count Orsino.

I recognise you

ANTONIO You do mistake me, sir.

1ST OFFICER No, sir, no jot. I know your favour well,
Though now you have no sea-cap on your head.
Take him away; he knows I know him well.

ANTONIO I must obey. *[To Viola]* This comes with seeking you.
But there's no remedy; I shall answer it.
What will you do, now my necessity
Makes me to ask you for my purse? It grieves me
Much more for what I cannot do for you
Than what befalls myself. You stand amazed,
But be of comfort.

tricky situation

2ND OFFICER Come, sir, away.

ANTONIO I must entreat of you some of that money.

VIOLA What money, sir?
For the fair kindness you have showed me here,
And part being prompted by your present trouble,
Out of my lean and low ability
I'll lend you something. My having is not much;
I'll make division of my present with you.
Hold, there's half my coffer. *[Offers him money]*

320-22 'I haven't got much, but I'll split what I've got on me with you. Look, here's half what's in my purse.'

ANTONIO Will you deny me now? *[Refuses it]*
Is't possible that my deserts to you
Can lack persuasion? Do not tempt my misery,
Lest that it make me so unsound a man
As to upbraid you with those kindnesses
That I have done for you.

324-8 'How is it I can't persuade you to help when you owe me so much? Don't make me miserable — I'll end up reminding you of everything I've done for you.'

VIOLA I know of none,
Nor know I you by voice or any feature.
I hate ingratitude more in a man
Than lying, vainness, babbling drunkenness,
Or any taint of vice whose strong corruption
Inhabits our frail blood.

330-33 'I hate ingratitude more than any of the vices which infect us.'

ANTONIO O heavens themselves!

2ND OFFICER Come, sir, I pray you go.

ANTONIO Let me speak a little. This youth that you see here,
I snatched one-half out of the jaws of death,

337-9 I 'saved him with feelings of holy love, and worshipped his image — I thought he would be worthy of it.'

Relieved him with such sanctity of love;
And to his image, which methought did promise
Most venerable worth, did I devotion.

1ST OFFICER What's that to us? The time goes by. Away!

ANTONIO But O how vile an idol proves this god!
Thou hast, Sebastian, done good feature shame.
In nature there's no blemish but the mind:
None can be called deformed but the unkind.
Virtue is beauty, but the beauteous-evil
Are empty trunks, o'er-flourished by the devil.

345-6 'beautiful people with evil characters are just hollow shells, made pretty by the devil.'

1ST OFFICER The man grows mad. Away with him! Come, come, sir.

ANTONIO Lead me on. *Exit [with Officers]*

VIOLA Methinks his words do from such passion fly
That he believes himself; so do not I.
Prove true, imagination, O prove true,
That I, dear brother, be now ta'en for you!

taken

SIR TOBY Come hither, knight, come hither, Fabian. We'll whisper o'er a couplet or two of most sage saws.

wise proverbs

VIOLA He named Sebastian. I my brother know
Yet living in my glass; even such and so
In favour was my brother, and he went
Still in this fashion, colour, ornament,
For him I imitate. O if it prove,
Tempests are kind, and salt waves fresh in love. *[Exit]*

356-8 'I see my brother every time I look in the mirror; this is how he looked'

SIR TOBY A very dishonest paltry boy, and more a coward than a hare; his dishonesty appears in leaving his friend here in necessity, and denying him; and for his cowardship, ask Fabian.

cheap

FABIAN A coward, a most devout coward, religious in it.

SIR ANDREW 'Slid, I'll after him again and beat him.

By God's eyelid!

SIR TOBY Do, cuff him soundly, but never draw thy sword.

SIR ANDREW And I do not – *[Exit]*

FABIAN Come, let's see the event.

SIR TOBY I dare lay any money, 'twill be nothing yet. *Exeunt*

371 'I'll bet you any money that nothing will come of it.'

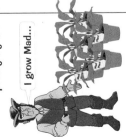

ACT 5 SCENE 1
Olivia's garden

In the final scene all the confusion gets cleared up, and they all live happily ever after — well sort of.

Enter FESTE and FABIAN

FABIAN Now, as thou lov'st me, let me see his letter.

FESTE Good Master Fabian, grant me another request.

1 'If you love me let me see Malvolio's letter.'

FABIAN Anything.

FESTE Do not desire to see this letter.

FABIAN This is to give a dog and in recompense desire my dog again.

5-6 'That's like giving me a dog, then asking for it back again.'

Enter ORSINO, VIOLA, CURIO, and Lords

ORSINO Belong you to the Lady Olivia, friends?

7 'Do you work for Lady Olivia?'

FESTE Ay, sir, we are some of her trappings.

accessories

ORSINO I know thee well. How dost thou, my good fellow?

FESTE Truly, sir, the better for my foes, and the worse for my friends.

enemies

ORSINO Just the contrary: the better for thy friends.

FESTE No, sir, the worse.

ORSINO How can that be?

FESTE Marry, sir, they praise me, and make an ass of me. Now my foes tell me plainly I am an ass, so that by my foes, sir, I profit in the knowledge of myself, and by my friends I am abused. So that, conclusions to be as kisses, if your four negatives make your two affirmatives, why then, the worse for my friends and the better for my foes.

15 'My friends praise me too much — it makes me look stupid.'

18-19 'Four negatives make two positives.'

ORSINO Why, this is excellent.

FESTE By my troth, sir, no, though it please you to be one of my friends.

22-3 'On my honour, it's not — even if you are my friend.'

ORSINO Thou shalt not be the worse for me: there's gold.

FESTE But that it would be double-dealing, sir, I would you could make it another.

giving twice *or* cheating

ORSINO O you give me ill counsel.

27 'You give me bad advice'.

FESTE Put your grace in your pocket, sir, for this once, and let your flesh and blood obey it.

28-9 'Ignore your noble character, and let yourself obey my advice.'

ORSINO Well, I will be so much a sinner to be a double-dealer: there's another.

FESTE *Primo, secundo, tertio,* is a good play, and the old saying is, 'The third pays for all'; the triplex, sir, is a good tripping measure; or the bells of Saint Bennet, sir, may put you in mind — one, two, three.

32 '*Primo, secundo, tertio*' is Latin for 'First, second, third'.

33 'Triplex' is a one-two-three dance rhythm.

ORSINO You can fool no more money out of me at this throw. If you will let your lady know I am here to speak with her, and bring her along with you, it may awake my bounty further.

this time around

37-9 'Get Olivia to come out here and I might feel more generous.'

FESTE Marry, sir, lullaby to your bounty till I come again. I go, sir, but I would not have you to think that my desire of having is the sin of covetousness; but, as you say, sir, let your bounty take a nap. I will awake it anon. *Exit*

greed

VIOLA Here comes the man, sir, that did rescue me.

Enter ANTONIO *and* OFFICERS

ORSINO That face of his I do remember well;
Yet when I saw it last, it was besmeared
As black as Vulcan, in the smoke of war.
A baubling vessel was he captain of,
For shallow draught and bulk unprizable,
With which, such scathful grapple did he make
With the most noble bottom of our fleet,
That very envy, and the tongue of loss,
Cried fame and honour on him. What's the matter?

the gods' blacksmith in Roman myths

48-53 'He was captain of a worthless little ship, but he caused our finest vessel such damage that envy itself praised him.'

What's going on?

1ST OFFICER Orsino, this is that Antonio
That took the Phoenix and her fraught from Candy,
And this is he that did the Tiger board,
When your young nephew Titus lost his leg.
Here in the streets, desperate of shame and state,
In private brabble did we apprehend him.

freight from Crete

58-9 'We caught him brawling in the street, as though he couldn't care less about his reputation.'

VIOLA He did me kindness, sir, drew on my side,
But in conclusion put strange speech upon me,
I know not what 'twas, but distraction.

60-62 'He drew his sword to help me, but then he spoke in a strange way — I don't know what it was, unless he was mad.'

ORSINO Notable pirate! Thou salt-water thief,
What foolish boldness brought thee to their mercies,
Whom thou, in terms so bloody and so dear,
Hast made thine enemies?

64-6 'What on earth are you doing here, where you've made such bitter enemies?'

ANTONIO Orsino, noble sir,
Be pleas'd that I shake off these names you give me:
Antonio never yet was thief or pirate,
Though I confess, on base and ground enough,
Orsino's enemy. A witchcraft drew me hither:
That most ungrateful boy there by your side,
From the rude sea's enraged and foamy mouth
Did I redeem. A wrack past hope he was.
His life I gave him, and did thereto add
My love without retention, or restraint,
All his in dedication. For his sake,
Did I expose myself, pure for his love,
Into the danger of this adverse town,
Drew to defend him when he was beset;
Where being apprehended, his false cunning
(Not meaning to partake with me in danger)
Taught him to face me out of his acquaintance,
And grew a twenty years' removèd thing
While one would wink; denied me mine own purse,
Which I had recommended to his use
Not half an hour before.

with good reason

save

76-78 'I came to this enemy town for Sebastian's sake, because I love him.'

80-84 'When I was arrested he didn't want to share my troubles, and all of a sudden pretended he'd never met me.'

lent him

VIOLA How can this be?
ORSINO When came he to this town?
ANTONIO Today, my lord, and for three months before,
No interim, not a minute's vacancy,
Both day and night did we keep company.

break

moment apart

Enter OLIVIA *and* ATTENDANTS

ORSINO Here comes the countess; now heaven walks on earth.
But for thee, fellow – Fellow, thy words are madness.
Three months this youth hath tended upon me,
But more of that anon. Take him aside.

93 'This boy's been looking after me for three months.'

OLIVIA What would my lord, but that he may not have,
Wherein Olivia may seem serviceable?
Cesario, you do not keep promise with me.

95-6 'Is there any favour I can do you (apart from the one I can't)?'

VIOLA Madam!
ORSINO Gracious Olivia –
OLIVIA What do you say, Cesario? Good my lord –
VIOLA My lord would speak; my duty hushes me.
OLIVIA If it be aught to the old tune, my lord,
It is as fat and fulsome to mine ear
As howling after music.

102-4 'If you say anything you've said before I'll find it as ugly as howling after music.'

ORSINO Still so cruel?
OLIVIA Still so constant, lord.
ORSINO What, to perverseness? You uncivil lady,
To whose ingrate and unauspicious altars
My soul the faithfull'st offerings have breathed out
That e'er devotion tendered! What shall I do?

106-9 'Constant to pig-headedness? Rude woman — I've offered you so much, but you're still ungrateful! What more can I do?'

OLIVIA Even what it please my lord that shall become him.

110 'Do whatever you think suits you.'

ORSINO Why should I not – had I the heart to do it –
Like to th' Egyptian thief at point of death
Kill what I love – a savage jealousy
That sometimes savours nobly? But hear me this.
Since you to non-regardance cast my faith,
And that I partly know the instrument
That screws me from my true place in your favour,
Live you the marble-breasted tyrant still.
But this your minion, whom I know you love,
And whom, by heaven I swear, I tender dearly,
Him will I tear out of that cruel eye
Where he sits crownèd in his master's spite.
Come, boy, with me; my thoughts are ripe in mischief.
I'll sacrifice the lamb that I do love,
To spite a raven's heart within a dove. *[Leaving]*

feels right

115-18 'Seeing as you don't care that I love you (and I know who's to blame), just carry on being cruel and cold-hearted.'

119-22 'As for your little darling, I'll take him away from you. He enjoys your love in spite of me, his master.'

VIOLA And I most jocund, apt, and willingly,
To do you rest, a thousand deaths would die. *[Following]*
OLIVIA Where goes Cesario?
VIOLA After him I love
More than I love these eyes, more than my life,

126-7 'I'd happily die a thousand times over, to put your mind at rest.'

More, by all mores, than e'er I shall love wife.
If I do feign, you witnesses above
Punish my life for tainting of my love!

OLIVIA Ay me, detested! How am I beguiled!
VIOLA Who does beguile you? Who does do you wrong?
OLIVIA Hast thou forgot thyself? Is it so long?
Call forth the holy father. *[Exit an Attendant]*
ORSINO Come, away!
OLIVIA Whither, my lord? Cesario, husband, stay!
ORSINO Husband?
OLIVIA Ay, husband. Can he that deny?
ORSINO Her husband, sirrah?
VIOLA No, my lord, not I.
OLIVIA Alas, it is the baseness of thy fear
That makes thee strangle thy propriety.
Fear not, Cesario, take thy fortunes up;
Be that thou know'st thou art, and then thou art
As great as that thou fear'st.

Enter PRIEST

O welcome, father!
Father, I charge thee by thy reverence
Here to unfold – though lately we intended
To keep in darkness what occasion now
Reveals before 'tis ripe – what thou dost know
Hath newly passed between this youth and me.

PRIEST A contract of eternal bond of love,
Confirmed by mutual joinder of your hands,
Attested by the holy close of lips,
Strengthened by th' interchangement of your rings,
And all the ceremony of this compact
Sealed in my function, by my testimony;
Since when, my watch hath told me, toward my grave
I have travelled but two hours.

ORSINO *[To Viola]* O, thou dissembling cub! What wilt thou be
When time hath sowed a grizzle on thy case?
Or will not else thy craft so quickly grow
That thine own trip shall be thine overthrow?
Farewell, and take her, but direct thy feet
Where thou and I henceforth may never meet.

VIOLA My lord, I do protest –
OLIVIA O, do not swear!
Hold little faith, though thou hast too much fear.

Enter SIR ANDREW *[his head bleeding]*

SIR ANDREW For the love of God, a surgeon! Send one presently to Sir Toby.
OLIVIA What's the matter?
SIR ANDREW H'as broke my head across, and has given Sir Toby a bloody coxcomb, too. For the love of God, your help! I had rather than forty pound I were at home.
OLIVIA Who has done this, Sir Andrew?
SIR ANDREW The count's gentleman, one Cesario. We took him for a coward, but he's the very devil incardinate.
ORSINO My gentleman Cesario?
SIR ANDREW Od's lifelings, here he is! You broke my head for nothing, and that that I did, I was set on to do't by Sir Toby.
VIOLA Why do you speak to me? I never hurt you.
You drew your sword upon me without cause,
But I bespake you fair, and hurt you not.

Enter SIR TOBY *and* CLOWN [FESTE]

SIR ANDREW If a bloody coxcomb be a hurt, you have hurt me; I think you set nothing by a bloody coxcomb. Here comes Sir Toby halting – you shall hear more; but if he had not been in drink, he would have tickled you othergates than he did.
ORSINO How now, gentleman? How is't with you?
SIR TOBY That's all one. H'as hurt me, and there's th' end on't. Sot, didst see Dick surgeon, sot?
FESTE O, he's drunk, Sir Toby, an hour agone; his eyes were set at eight i' th' morning.
SIR TOBY Then he's a rogue, and a passy-measures pavin. I hate a drunken rogue.
OLIVIA Away with him! Who hath made this havoc with them?
SIR ANDREW I'll help you, Sir Toby, because we'll be dressed together.
SIR TOBY Will you help? – an ass-head, and a coxcomb, and a knave, a thin-faced knave, a gull?
OLIVIA Get him to bed, and let his hurt be looked to.

[Exeunt Feste, Fabian, Sir Toby, and Sir Andrew]

Enter SEBASTIAN

SEBASTIAN I am sorry, madam, I have hurt your kinsman.
But had it been the brother of my blood,
I must have done no less with wit and safety.
You throw a strange regard upon me, and by that
I do perceive it hath offended you.
Pardon me, sweet one, even for the vows
We made each other but so late ago.

ORSINO One face, one voice, one habit, and two persons
A natural perspective, that is and is not!
SEBASTIAN Antonio! O, my dear Antonio,
How have the hours racked and tortured me,
Since I have lost thee!
ANTONIO Sebastian are you?
SEBASTIAN Fear'st thou that, Antonio?
ANTONIO How have you made division of yourself?

131-2 'If I'm faking, let the gods above punish me for cheapening my love!'

put upon

priest

hide your identity

140-44 'You're afraid to say what you've done in front of Orsino. Don't be afraid. Admit it and you'll have no need to be afraid — being married to me makes you his equal.'

145-49 'You'd better explain what this boy and I have done — even though we planned to keep it a secret.'

joining

proved

promise

155 'I'm a genuine priest so it's all guaranteed'

158-61 'You lying cub! What will you be like when you're grey-haired? Or will you get so cunning that your own tricks ruin you.'

Rats!

now

he's the devil himself

By God!

176-7 'You cracked my skull for no reason. I only did what I did because Sir Toby put me up to it.'

spoke to you in friendly way

head

limping

183-5 'if Sir Toby hadn't been drunk he would have given you a real hiding.'

old drunk

189-90 'He was dead drunk by eight this morning.'

a slow, swaying dance

bandaged

I've got a cock's comb too.

Show-off.

199-200 'Even if he'd been my own brother, it would have been the sensible and safe thing to do.'

mirror which makes double reflections

205-6 'The same face, voice and clothes, but on two people. It's a real-life illusion — true and false at the same time!'

211 'How have you split yourself in two?'

212-13 'These two look more alike than the halves of an apple.'

An apple cleft in two is not more twin
Than these two creatures. Which is Sebastian?

OLIVIA Most wonderful!

SEBASTIAN Do I stand there? I never had a brother;
Nor can there be that deity in my nature
Of here and everywhere. I had a sister,
Whom the blind waves and surges have devoured.
Of charity, what kin are you to me?
What countryman? What name? What parentage?

216-17 'I haven't got magical powers to be in two places at once.'

For pity's sake

Now I'm confused.

dressed

VIOLA Of Messaline. Sebastian was my father;
Such a Sebastian was my brother, too;
So went he suited to his watery tomb.
If spirits can assume both form and suit,
You come to fright us.

SEBASTIAN A spirit I am indeed,
But am in that dimension grossly clad
Which from the womb I did participate.
Were you a woman – as the rest goes even –
I should my tears let fall upon your cheek,
And say, 'Thrice welcome, drownèd Viola.'

225-7 'I am a sort of spirit, but still housed in the solid body I was born in.'

VIOLA My father had a mole upon his brow.

SEBASTIAN And so had mine.

VIOLA And died that day when Viola from her birth
Had numbered thirteen years.

233-4 'He died on Viola's thirteenth birthday.'

SEBASTIAN O, that record is lively in my soul!
He finishèd indeed his mortal act
That day that made my sister thirteen years.

memory

died

VIOLA If nothing lets to make us happy both,
But this my masculine usurped attire,
Do not embrace me, till each circumstance,
Of place, time, fortune, do cohere and jump
That I am Viola, which to confirm
I'll bring you to a captain in this town,
Where lie my maiden weeds; by whose gentle help
I was preserved – to serve this noble count.
All the occurrence of my fortune since
Hath been between this lady and this lord.

238-42 'If the only thing to stop us being happy is these men's clothes, wait till everything proves I am Viola before you embrace me.'

girl's clothes

246-7 'Everything that's happened to me since, has had to do with this lady and this lord.'

SEBASTIAN *[To Olivia]* So comes it, lady, you have been mistook.
But nature to her bias drew in that.
You would have been contracted to a maid;
Nor are you therein, by my life, deceived;
You are betrothed both to a maid and man.

engaged to a girl, i.e. Viola

248-9 'It turns out you've made a mistake. But nature made sure you would.'

virgin, i.e. Sebastian

ORSINO Be not amazed, right noble is his blood.
If this be so – as yet the glass seems true –
I shall have share in this most happy wreck.
[To Viola] Boy, thou hast said to me a thousand times
Thou never shouldst love woman like to me.

253-5 'Don't be upset, he's got noble blood. If all this is really true, I'll have a share of this happy accident.'

VIOLA And all those sayings will I over-swear,
And all those swearings keep as true in soul
As doth that orbèd continent the fire
That severs day from night.

swear again

259-61 'I'll keep my oaths as pure as the fire of the sun.'

ORSINO Give me thy hand;
And let me see thee in thy woman's weeds.

VIOLA The captain that did bring me first on shore
Hath my maid's garments; he upon some action
Is now in durance, at Malvolio's suit,
A gentleman and follower of my lady's.

264-5 'The Captain's in prison — he's being sued by Malvolio.'

OLIVIA He shall enlarge him; fetch Malvolio hither.
And yet, alas, now I remember me,
They say, poor gentleman, he's much distract.

let him go

gone completely potty

Enter CLOWN [FESTE], *with a letter, and* FABIAN

A most extracting frenzy of mine own
From my remembrance clearly banished his.
How does he, sirrah?

270-71 'I was feeling quite mad myself, and it made me forget about Malvolio.'

FESTE Truly, madam, he holds Belzebub at the stave's end as well as a man in his case may do; h'as here writ a letter to you; I should have given't you today morning. But as a madman's epistles are no gospels, so it skills not much when they are delivered.

273-4 'Madam, he's holding back the devil as best he can.'

276-7 'A madman's letters aren't gospel-truth, so it doesn't matter when they're delivered.'

OLIVIA Open't, and read it.

FESTE Look then to be well edified when the fool delivers the madman. *[Reads madly]* 'By the Lord, madam –'

279-80 'You're sure to learn a lot when a fool speaks for a madman.'

OLIVIA How now, art thou mad?

FESTE No, madam, I do but read madness; and your ladyship will have it as it ought to be, you must allow *vox.*

let me read it in character

OLIVIA Prithee read i' thy right wits.

FESTE So I do, madonna; but to read his right wits is to read thus. Therefore, perpend, my princess, and give ear.

perpend sort of means pay attention — but it's not a real word

OLIVIA *[To Fabian]* Read it you, sirrah.

FABIAN *[Reads]* 'By the Lord, madam, you wrong me, and the world shall know it. Though you have put me into darkness, and given your drunken cousin rule over me, yet have I the benefit of my senses as well as your ladyship. I have your own letter that induced me to the semblance I put on; with the which I doubt not but to do myself much right, or you much shame. Think of me as you please. I leave my duty a little unthought of and speak out of my injury.
The madly used Malvolio.'

290-92 'I'm in my right mind as much as you are. I've got your letter, which told me to put on an act.'

He's maaad!

OLIVIA Did he write this?

FESTE Ay, madam.

ORSINO This savours not much of distraction.

299 'That doesn't sound very mad.'

OLIVIA See him delivered, Fabian; bring him hither. *[Exit Fabian]*
My lord, so please you, these things further thought on,
To think me as well a sister as a wife,
One day shall crown th' alliance on't, so please you,
Here at my house, and at my proper cost.

released

301-4 'Orsino, if you can think of me as a sister instead of a wife, we could celebrate our weddings together, at my house — and I'll pay.'

ORSINO Madam, I am most apt t' embrace your offer.
[To Viola] Your master quits you; and for your service done him,
So much against the mettle of your sex,
So far beneath your soft and tender breeding,
And since you called me master for so long,
Here is my hand; you shall from this time be
Your master's mistress.
OLIVIA A sister! You are she.

Enter [FABIAN *with*] MALVOLIO

ORSINO Is this the madman?
OLIVIA Ay, my lord, this same.
How now, Malvolio?
MALVOLIO Madam, you have done me wrong,
Notorious wrong.
OLIVIA Have I, Malvolio? No.
MALVOLIO Lady, you have. Pray you, peruse that letter.
You must not now deny it is your hand;
Write from it, if you can, in hand, or phrase,
Or say 'tis not your seal, not your invention.
You can say none of this. Well, grant it then,
And tell me, in the modesty of honour,
Why you have given me such clear lights of favour,
Bade me come smiling and cross-gartered to you,
To put on yellow stockings, and to frown
Upon Sir Toby, and the lighter people;
And acting this in an obedient hope,
Why have you suffered me to be imprisoned,
Kept in a dark house, visited by the priest,
And made the most notorious geck and gull,
That e'er invention played on? Tell me, why?
OLIVIA Alas, Malvolio, this is not my writing,
Though I confess much like the character.
But, out of question, 'tis Maria's hand.
And now I do bethink me, it was she
First told me thou wast mad; then cam'st in smiling,
And in such forms which here were presupposed
Upon thee in the letter. Prithee, be content;
This practice hath most shrewdly passed upon thee;
But when we know the grounds, and authors of it,
Thou shalt be both the plaintiff and the judge
Of thine own cause.
FABIAN Good madam, hear me speak,
And let no quarrel, nor no brawl to come,
Taint the condition of this present hour,
Which I have wondered at. In hope it shall not,
Most freely I confess, myself and Toby
Set this device against Malvolio here,
Upon some stubborn and uncourteous parts
We had conceived against him. Maria writ
The letter, at Sir Toby's great importance,
In recompense whereof he hath married her.
How with a sportful malice it was followed
May rather pluck on laughter than revenge,
If that the injuries be justly weighed,
That have on both sides passed.
OLIVIA Alas, poor fool, how have they baffled thee!
FESTE Why, 'Some are born great, some achieve greatness, and some have greatness thrown upon them.' I was one, sir, in this interlude, one Sir Topas, sir – but that's all one. 'By the Lord, fool, I am not mad.' But do you remember – 'Madam, why laugh you at such a barren rascal, and you smile not, he's gagged'? And thus the whirligig of time brings in his revenges.
MALVOLIO I'll be revenged on the whole pack of you! [Exit]
OLIVIA He hath been most notoriously abused.
ORSINO Pursue him, and entreat him to a peace.
He hath not told us of the captain yet. [Exit Fabian]
When that is known, and golden time convents,
A solemn combination shall be made
Of our dear souls. Meantime, sweet sister,
We will not part from hence. Cesario, come –
For so you shall be while you are a man,
But when in other habits you are seen,
Orsino's mistress, and his fancy's queen.

Exeunt [all but Feste]

FESTE [sings]
When that I was and a little tiny boy,
With hey, ho, the wind and the rain,
A foolish thing was but a toy,
For the rain it raineth every day.
But when I came to man's estate,
With hey, ho, the wind and the rain,
'Gainst knaves and thieves men shut their gate,
For the rain it raineth every day.
But when I came, alas, to wive,
With hey, ho, the wind and the rain,
By swaggering could I never thrive,
For the rain it raineth every day.
But when I came unto my beds,
With hey, ho, the wind and the rain,
With tosspots still 'had drunken heads,
For the rain it raineth every day.
A great while ago the world begun,
With hey, ho, the wind and the rain,
But that's all one, our play is done,
And we'll strive to please you every day.

305 'I'm delighted to accept your offer.'

nature
terrible
read
handwriting
writing style
servants
allowed
twit and twerp
trick

330-32 'It looks like my handwriting, but it's definitely Maria's.'

you came
suggested to you

337-40 'The trick worked really well on you, but when we know who thought it up, and why, you can defend yourself, and judge them.'

340-47 'I don't want the moment ruined with quarrels so I'll admit that Toby and I set up the trick after Malvolio

insistence
repayment

350-53 'If you knew the wrongs on both sides you'd laugh at the trick not want revenge.'

made a mockery of you
episode
but, who cares?
unfunny fool

360-61 'Time passes like a spinning top, and brings revenge.'

beg him to make peace

366-8 'When we have heard about the captain, and golden time brings us together, our souls will be joined in marriage.'

clothes

375 'Foolish behaviour was just a game.'

377 'When I grew up'

379 'I was rejected as a scoundrel and a thief'

showing off

385 'When I got old'

387 'I was still drinking with the other boozers'

Just me left, then.

Index

Index